LETTERS TO MY GRANDCHILDREN

Tony Benn

LETTERS TO MY GRANDCHILDREN

HUTCHINSON

LONDON

Published by Hutchinson 2009

2 4 6 8 10 9 7 5 3 1

Copyright © Tony Benn 2009

Author has asserted his right under the Copyright, Designs
and Patents Act 1988 to be identified as the author of this work

First published in Great Britain in 2009 by
Hutchinson
Random House, 20 Vauxhall Bridge Road,
London SW1V 2SA

www.rbooks.co.uk

Addresses for companies within The Random House Group Limited can
be found at: www.randomhouse.co.uk/offices.htm

The Random House Group Limited Reg. No. 954009

A CIP catalogue record for this book
is available from the British Library

ISBN 9780091931261

The Random House Group Limited supports The Forest Stewardship
Council (FSC), the leading international forest certification organisation.
All our titles that are printed on Greenpeace approved FSC certified paper
carry the FSC logo. Our paper procurement policy can be found at
www.rbooks.co.uk/environment

Mixed Sources
Product group from well-managed
forests and other controlled sources
www.fsc.org Cert no. TT-COC-2139
© 1996 Forest Stewardship Council
FSC

Typeset in Adobe Caslon by
Palimpsest Book Production Limited,
Grangemouth, Stirlingshire

Printed in the UK by
CPI Mackays, Chatham ME5 8TD

LETTERS

ACKNOWLEDGEMENTS

I am deeply grateful to Hutchinson for agreeing to publish this book and in particular to Tony Whittome, who has encouraged me throughout and devoted a great deal of his attention to the form the book should take.

My main debt, however, is owed to Ruth Winstone, who has edited twelve of my books along with many films and videos.

In this book she organised my disparate thoughts into a series of letters which I hope will make sense to the reader.

Ruth is my very best friend and I trust her judgement completely.

Tony Benn
3 April 2009

Letters to my Grandchildren

Tony BENN

Dear Nahal, Michael, James, William, Jonathan, Caroline, Emily, Daniel, Hannah and Sarah,

I am very proud of you all. The oldest of you is now thirty one and the youngest thirteen, and you are all fit, healthy and bright, and that is all that grandparents can wish for. I am just sorry that Grandma did not live to see you all grow up.

Long before you were born, when your parents were still small, I was a busy MP and I did not spend as much time with them as I should have. To expiate my guilt I wrote a story for them, 'The Daddy Shop', which I will add as a postscript for your amusement, at the end of this book.

It is hard to believe that four of you were born in the 1980s, children of the Thatcher era, and the youngest in the first days of New Labour.

You now live in a dangerous world, and my concern for you all – and indeed the whole younger generation – is very simple.

It is that the future of the human race is in your hands and you have to make some of the biggest choices ever to be faced by mankind.

Now that chemical, nuclear and biological weapons are so widespread, yours is one of the first generations in human history with the power to destroy the human race.

One man can be killed with a sword or a bow and arrow, a few more with a machine gun, a lot with a bomb; but now the scale of possible destruction is unimaginable.

Yours is also the first generation that has at its disposal the technology, the know-how and the money to solve humanity's basic needs. And that has never been true before. People have always dreamed of a world of peace and plenty but it was beyond man's capacity to secure it. With a population expected soon to be 9 billion you must decide how to share the finite resources of the planet.

My generation has failed yours. In thirty-one years, from 1914 to 1945, 105 million people were killed in two European wars, and many more injured, using conventional weapons – save only for Hiroshima and Nagasaki where atomic bombs spread devastation and hundreds of thousands died.

In 1983 I visited Hiroshima. The most moving moment was when my guide pointed to a small dark mark on the kerbside where a child had been sitting when the atomic bomb landed.

The child's body had been vaporised by the intense heat. Next to the dark mark was a twisted metal lunch box that had belonged to the child.

The bomb could not vaporise the lunch box but it was contorted into a hideous shape and that was all there was to commemorate the death of an innocent being: the mark and the lunch box.

I shall never forget it.

Then came the Cold War between the capitalist and the communist countries, and the disastrous arms race.

Fears of nuclear proliferation and destruction dominated the latter half of the twentieth century. Now, in the twenty-first, new dangers and threats – potentially as serious – have arisen.

The inexorable tide of economic growth and consumerism has taken its toll of the planet. Environmentalists have warned us that climate change will produce catastrophic flooding; the existence of whole species is threatened through the loss of their habitat, or from man's greed; religious extremism whether Christian, Zionist or Islamic is used to justify violence and murder; and new diseases and risks – AIDS and obesity – have taken the place of earlier ones such as polio and TB.

What are your fears, hopes and expectations as you look into the future? What are the problems which you would want to tackle? And how?

I have made many mistakes, and I have also become aware as I have got older how little I know. I am much less sure than I was in my youth that I am right about anything and for these reasons I am reluctant to give advice to you.

Today's world – so different from the world in which I was born – is something you take for granted. It was there when you were born and normality is the world one enters into at birth.

As a silver surfer struggling with the internet, I have long since learned that when my laptop crashes one of you, a grandson or granddaughter, will turn up, press two buttons and get me back online.

Just to put recent advances in perspective: when your great-great-great-grandfather James Holmes was born in 1831 only 2 per cent of the population could vote, and Stephenson's Rocket had not yet launched the era of rail. When your great-great-grandfather John Benn was born in 1850 there were no telephones in use. When your great-grandmother (my mother) Margaret Holmes was born in

1897 women did not have the vote and no aircraft had ever left the surface of the earth. Even when your grandfather (that's me!) was born there was no television, and when your parents were born in the 1950s computers were not in general use and the internet had not been developed.

It is tempting to try to imagine what technology will exist when *your* grandchildren are eighty-four (my age now) in 2125. But one thing is sure. The choices they face could be even more challenging than those which you face.

One thing has not changed over the centuries and that is the moral principle which should guide us in life. The founders of the world's religions taught us that we should treat people as we expect to be treated ourselves. It is also the message of trade union banners – 'An injury to one is an injury to all'.

Every generation has to fight the same battles for peace, justice and democracy, and there is no *final* victory nor *final* defeat. Your generation will have to take up its own battles.

These are the ideas which led me to write this book, and I address them to you but also to your generation in the hope that they give you all encouragement to develop ways of safeguarding mankind and making life better for humanity.

With love

Your devoted grandfather,
Dan Dan

When your parents were your age, and the United States and the Soviet Union were racing to land on the moon, the Russians put down a little robotic machine onto the lunar surface.

One of my constituents in Bristol, where I was then the MP, wrote to me:

> Dear Tony,
> I see the Russians have put a space vehicle on the moon. Is there any chance of a better bus service in Bristol?

It was a very good question.

From the beginning of time to the days when your future great-grandchildren are born, the choice is and will always be: what do you do with the technology you have? Is it for peace or war? Does it divide people or help to bring them together? And what effect could it have on the human race's capacity to govern itself peacefully?

The uses made of technology thus raise fundamental moral issues.

In that sense the teachings of Jesus are more relevant now because the stakes are higher, and the violent anti-Christian atheists who denounce those who follow Jesus completely fail to appreciate that science and technology offer no moral guidance as to what should be done with them. And yet it is the moral guidance that is needed more than ever, because the world is literally one small community locked together.

When as a minister I was visiting Kiev (then in the Soviet Union), I met a Soviet cyberneticist, Academician Glushkov, who said to me, 'There have been three great revolutions in recent years: nuclear weapons, which frightened everybody; space exploration, which excited everybody; but the most important of all has gone almost unnoticed – the computer revolution, which has changed everything.'

He was absolutely right. It has been the revolution in communications that has completely transformed the world from being a gathering of nation states based upon the power struggles of the past into that interlocking community, Spaceship Earth. Therefore our fate will be determined collectively and it is for your generation to work out what that fate will be.

*G*randson *William* publishes an online satirical magazine called *Re:Spectacle*. It costs almost nothing – except his time – and depends a lot on his talented friends. He publishes what he likes and has no editor to censor or thwart his views or content.

All of you grandchildren, like everyone of your generation, take the internet and its social possibilities for granted. The technicalities of using it are hard for parents and grandparents to master but it has helped to create the best-informed generation in history and gives you freedom to exchange information and compare interests across the world.

This very fact has made it a deadly threat to the powerful.

Throughout history control of communication and information has been crucial to political control. Dictators use that power over information to dominate their people even if there is no provision for democracy.

The Church in the early days maintained its power because it was run by clerks who were literate; the Heresy Act of 1401 made it a criminal offence for a lay person to read the Bible. If anybody had an opportunity to study it, they could challenge the authority of the Pope.

Bishop Tyndale, the dissident Christian, lost his life and Mercator, the revolutionary map-maker, was imprisoned because they gave ordinary people the opportunity to challenge the information propagated by the powerful.

The power of the priesthood eventually came up against the secular power of the king and so Henry VIII nationalised the Church; the Anglican Church then exercised its new power by telling the faithful that God wanted the king to be king and, as church attendance was compulsory, this was a powerful instrument of control.

The Royal Mail was established in 1660 by Charles II, motivated in part, it is believed, by his desire to open his subjects' letters to find out if they were doing anything that might threaten his authority.

Luke Hansard, who gave his name to the reporting of parliament, was initially imprisoned for publishing its proceedings. Some courageous advocates for civil liberties and the freedom of the press have campaigned against restrictions – such as the Official Secrets Act – which prevent the public from knowing what governments are doing, while governments want to know what everyone else is doing.

With the growth of radio, the Conservative government of the day made broadcasting a public industry for the same reason that Henry VIII had taken over the Church.

The United States recognised the potential and importance of controlling information globally. When Bill Clinton was in the White House, the Pentagon issued a document called 'Full Spectrum Dominance', which stated that the US intended to establish control in space, land, sea, air and information, of which *information* was the most important.

The internet has potentially transformed all that, and your generation is already experiencing the results. Newspapers are losing circulation to the electronic media; half of all Britons read a daily paper now compared to three quarters thirty years ago. It is possible to organise international events – such as the Stop the War demonstrations and the G20 protests – on the same day in fifty or sixty countries. And information and opinion can be disseminated instant-aneously without the intermediate role of an editor or censor. This is already seen as a threat to established power, which is why China insisted that Google monitor the information it provided in China, and why an electronic *intifada* is being fought by the Palestinians in their struggle for justice; and why, it has been alleged, the CIA plant damaging informa-tion on Wikipedia about people whom they do not like.

I believe that the internet offers us the best hope ever of getting through to each other and challenging abuses of power, and I am absolutely confident that your generation will use technology – blogging, Facebook, YouTube and Twittering together with your mobile phones and digital cameras – more effectively than has ever been possible before in the eternal struggle for peace and justice.

Y*ou think nothing* of jumping on a plane and going to Beijing, or Nepal or Tehran. But when you arrive in any country, you should always ask yourself, 'Who runs the joint?'

Power in the world has always been exercised by a tiny handful of people with their gangs of followers, and it is very easy to see what their interests are – to hang on to their wealth and power and increase them wherever possible.

One obvious instrument of control is violence and force and its associated statutes; under slavery men, women and children were literally owned and controlled, and risked even death for disobedience.

Other people were controlled by the discipline of religion: if they disobeyed the priest they might be threatened with purgatory or permanent hell – or death – as a punishment for their rebellion. In Afghanistan today women are killed simply for their opposition to Sharia law.

In industrial society, workers are to some extent at the mercy of their employers and might be sacked if they oppose or question their conditions of employment; if they have a mortgage and cannot make the repayments, their homes may be repossessed. So debt slavery is also a form of control.

Of course, we believe slavery to have ended and imperialism to be history, but there are two new forms of slavery that have developed in your lifetime: the hideous trafficking of women for prostitution and the completely unacceptable use of child labour to produce cheap consumer goods for the richer countries. Imperialism continues, too, in the form of American power and European Union expansion and is emerging in China, where economic aggrandisement and population size will produce the next empire.

Given the injustice that still exists across the world, do you ever ask yourself: why do people put up with it?

The answer is that subtle mechanisms are used by established ruling elites to stave off opposition.

First, they keep people cowed with the fear of a dangerous enemy: in the first fifty years of the twentieth century, the Kaiser's Germany was held up as the enemy; then Hitler (who had been supported by Conservative governments before the war). Opposition to him was not based on the Nazi use of gas chambers but because it was thought he threatened British interests.

After 1945 Stalin became the enemy and billions of pounds were spent on weapons of war to prevent a possible Soviet invasion. In retrospect, it looks increasingly absurd to imagine that the Soviet Union would have invaded Europe or taken on NATO given that it had lost so many millions of men in the war. Now we know that the Soviet Union was not even able to win a war in Afghanistan or Chechnya.

In the twenty-first century new fears have arisen. Islamic fundamentalism is the enemy and Christian extremists such as President George W. Bush claimed to have been instructed by God to invade Iraq. Then there is a new anxiety about what used to be called 'the yellow peril', the supremacy of the Chinese, as the world's former dominant economy, the American, falls into deep crisis.

And there is fear in the West of immigration: of loss of identity, competition for jobs, shortage of housing.

But it is the 'war on terror' that has been most recently and most ruthlessly used to justify a massive erosion of civil liberties.

Another mechanism of control is to divide people: setting men against women and women against men; black against white and white against black; native-born against immigrant and new immigrant against old immigrant; and Christians, Muslims and Jews against each other.

Exaggerating these divisions – and acquiring power – involves finding scapegoats, as Hitler recognised in Germany.

And it tries to conceal the fact that all people of both sexes, all faiths and nationalities have a common interest in achieving justice. Unity among the poor would pose a grave threat to the rich, and the rich know it so people are encouraged to think of themselves in specific groupings which build a sense of identity but which in fact keep them apart from each other. We are English, or British, or Welsh or Scottish, or Tutsis, or Hutus, or Catholics, or Shia or Sunni. Actually the Marxist division into class – the exploited and the exploiters – is still the most important division.

A third method of control is achieved through demoralisation, by the suggestion that only an intellectual elite has the capacity or the entitlement to play a role in society. Educational selection is one way in which governments for many years claimed the right to decide at the age of eleven who was worth educating and who was not. The 'eleven-plus' still exists, either openly or more discreetly, in some schools.

The elaborate system of league tables, which replicate the competitive spirit of the economic market, is another example of demoralisation, as is the rating of hospitals. This struck me forcibly when I had my pacemaker installed in a hospital which was, according to the Department of Health, the worst in Britain. Can you imagine the effect that ranking had on everyone who worked there?

The final instrument of control is more subtly exercised: the encouragement of cynicism (which permeates the media), the feeling that the public services are run by incompetents and that members of parliament and ministers are all dishonest and in some way corrupt, a perception which members of parliament's exploitation of the allowances system has gone a long way to confirm.

If people had confidence in the democratic process they would realise its potential and use it to create a fairer and better society for themselves.

The poor can always outvote the rich. That, no doubt, is what Hitler believed when he wrote in *Mein Kampf* that 'democracy inevitably leads to Marxism'.

So successful have these four instruments of control been that large numbers of people have became pessimistic. We often speak of the corruption of power, but the phrase 'the corruption of the powerless' is also relevant for if people without power give up hope they are involuntarily consenting to what is being done to them and are thus contributors to their own fate.

The abuse by elected members of parliament of their position for the purposes of self-enrichment, and the antics of non-elected advisers which lower the debate to the level of the gutter only exacerbate the cynicism which is so corrosive of trust.

If you want a factual answer to a question, you Google and find it in a fraction of the time it would have taken me seventy years ago; and you can communicate with your friends across the globe instantaneously.

It is such a contrast to earlier generations, who had to use reference books, which became out of date almost immediately, who lived in villages, knew their parents, neighbours and school friends but rarely heard of any event outside their own community. Even in my generation most people stayed close to where they were born and lived with only a sketchy awareness of the wider cultural and social world.

Of course the information now available by these new means may be wrong or inaccurate, or planted to misinform, but that was also true of books, pamphlets and newspapers.

It is difficult to forecast the impact of this instantaneous information and communication on the future of your world but it is inconceivable that it will not have the most profound effect in widening horizons, extending understanding and spreading new ideas.

Nor are you just recipients of this information; blogging is growing at a fantastic rate and is virtually costless. It means that anyone can express their opinions on the internet and influence others; each blogger becomes a proprietor of his own newspaper without the influence of advertising (or the revenue it brings).

It goes without saying that this is real power and it is not surprising that some countries are nervous of the effect on their citizens, who had previously relied on official sources of information.

Hacking, which is a highly skilled hobby, has become a serious offence because bright youngsters can get into the secret files of the MOD or the Pentagon by leaping over the restrictions designed to protect the sites from interlopers.

The surveillance and interception of communications have become far more intrusive than ever before, and with that degree of knowledge about our thoughts and activities available to state authorities, the scope for blackmail is unlimited. I can imagine circumstances under which 'awkward' people would be warned that if they did not mend their ways, certain information held about them could be released into the public domain and cause them embarrassment.

Under more authoritarian governments with such weapons at their disposal you would discover, too late, that your privacy had been taken from you. Don't let it happen!

When you reached the age of eighteen – those of you who have – you became an employer of your local MP whether or not you voted for him or her, and that MP is answerable to you

I can think of no greater honour than serving as an MP, and the relationship between you and your MP must be one of trust, for in a democracy sovereignty belongs to the people and they merely lend their power to those who represent them. An MP's first responsibility is therefore to constituents.

The second responsibility of an MP is to the local party, who can select – and deselect – the candidate and must trust whoever they do select to work honestly for the policies to which they are committed.

MPs also have a general responsibility to the party of which they are members.

Finally and most importantly, MPs have a responsibility to their own conscience, which may on occasion lead them into conflict with their local or national party or even into voting against the majority opinion of their constituents.

Throughout my fifty years in parliament I have come to respect and trust the members of all parties who have done a conscientious job representing their electors and expressing their own convictions. Without trust the system would collapse; the parliamentary crisis of 2009 is a crisis of trust.

The revelations about MPs' expenses have inflicted huge damage, not only on certain MPs and parliament but on the democratic process itself. My views on the immediate question are simple.

First, the salaries and allowances that are necessarily granted to MPs to do their work must be laid down by a completely independent body.

Second, all expense claims must be made public when they are submitted so that any constituent or colleague can reach their own conclusion as to their validity. Publicity is the best disinfectant. Offers to repay some of their expenses by MPs who have been criticised would never have occurred if they had not been published.

Third, the register of members' interests which was established some years ago should be extended to become a register of candidates' interests, for electors are entitled to know the interests of all candidates *before* they are elected rather than after. This information should be available to all electors when they receive their polling card before an election.

All members of parliament should be required to publish their income-tax returns so that their other sources of income are known to their constituents and colleagues in parliament.

A cap should be imposed on the size of political contributions to all parties and candidates and the donations should be published before election day.

If all this were done the problems we face could in future be avoided and a relationship of trust re-established.

There is, of course, the wider question, best articulated by the Democrat Jack Gilligan, a former governor of Ohio, who said, 'You will never have democracy in America while big business buys both parties and expects a payoff whichever one wins.'

That remark, cynical as it may sound, does contain a very important truth, which is that power and money, skilfully used, can undermine the ballot box and deprive electors of a real choice when they vote.

It could well be argued that we have a one-party state in Britain. All our major parties support our possession of nuclear weapons, our membership of the European Union, our special relationship with America, the pre-eminence of private ownership and severe restrictions on trade unions.

There are, of course, fringe parties and candidates which may win a few seats in local authorities and even one or two in parliament, but they are not treated with respect by the editors of newspapers or political leaders because they lack the strength of numbers, even if their arguments are valid.

My father (your great-grandfather) was a Labour MP at a time when the party was still young. The party was established by the trade unions and socialists to challenge the monopoly of power exercised by the Liberals and Conservatives, who succeeded each other with only marginal differences in policy. It represented working people. New Labour, however, certainly has no real links with that Labour Party, and its policies followed on from those of Mrs Thatcher, which guaranteed it a good press and a succession of electoral victories.

The massive debt crisis that hit the world in 2008 was a crisis made inevitable by the policies followed during that thirty-year period from 1979. Given this situation, how do political parties re-establish their identity and win support?

The answer, it now appears, is by negative campaigning and tactics, including the use of personal smears against opponents in the hope that this will discourage the electorate from voting for them.

Personal smears are not new in politics and are intended to avoid real debate about policy; they guarantee newspaper circulation and are effective politically.

But the deliberate use of smears against individuals has now come to be associated with the strategy of New Labour; smears suggesting that Conservative leaders were guilty of actions that would make them unsuitable for office.

If New Labour is reduced to resorting to this low level of abuse, this raises very serious questions about Labour's integrity and paucity of policies and principles, in a country that is still at war, that has over 2 million unemployed and rising homelessness and poverty. Are we seriously to expect that electors will forget all that out of disgust at the personal life of a politician from another party?

Instead of being representative, politics has become a crude competitive struggle between two alternative management teams, each of which is ready to do whatever is necessary to discredit its competitors.

Having suffered myself from attacks of this kind which were very frightening and destabilising, I came to the conclusion that the best thing was to go on saying what I believed, take the flak and hope that people would listen in the end.

Democracy itself is at risk if the cynicism this creates were to persuade people that everyone involved in politics is corrupt and a fraud and none should be trusted. If the idea spreads that the whole political process is not about choice but about power, it is an invitation to far-right leaders who could come forward and promise that if they are entrusted with power they will clean up what Hitler called 'the filth of parliamentary democracy'.

In saying this I am not seeking to alarm you but rather to draw your attention to the enormously important choices you have to make, through elected representatives, and the importance of trust between governments and people which must be the foundation of a mature and secure democracy.

This is why, when I left parliament in 2001, I decided to concentrate on individual campaigns, judging the Labour Party in terms of its position on these particular issues.

Can Labour re-emerge as a political party that represents the aspirations of people for peace and jobs and freedom? And if not, what will replace it?

As you all know, I have been a member of the Labour Party since I was seventeen. I am well aware how much I owe to the party and have a genuine affection and regard for its achievements and the people who have made them possible. But if, as a result of the 2010 general election, a coalition were to be formed in which New Labour agreed to take part, it would reawaken memories of Ramsay MacDonald's national government of 1931, which nearly destroyed the Labour Party and left it with only fifty MPs in the new parliament.

The priority now is to make demands on this and future governments and build strong extra-parliamentary connections across the political spectrum.

That is what the People's Charter, launched in 2009 by trade unions and Labour activists, is all about. It mirrors the famous Chartist petition of 1838, with six principles: a fairer economy for a fairer Britain; more and better jobs;

decent homes for all; save and improve public services; a fair and just Britain; a future without war.

If these demands are clearly formulated in terms of policy, win wide popular support and are pressed for with sufficient determination, no government can ignore them. I think that is exactly what is needed at this time in the history of the Labour Party, which has played such an important role in our family's life.

Every night when I go to bed I am relatively more ignorant than when I got up that morning, because the growth of human knowledge is so great I cannot keep up with it. I define this as the principle of progressive relative ignorance, and speaking at university graduations I always say, 'When you leave this university you will know far less that there is to be known than when you arrived.'

Professors look alarmed, but it is true. It induces a proper modesty and highlights the importance of finding the facts for yourself and thinking about them.

I have realised over the years that I am in the oral tradition. I have learned almost everything by listening and watching the reaction of an audience to what I say. One of the most interesting aspects of being an MP is how much you learn from listening – in discussions and from the weekly surgery or advice centre.

For over fifty-one years, nearly every Friday I would sit listening to people with problems which I might be able to help with.

Letters came in their hundreds of thousands but were much less vivid than the spoken word. The relationship between an MP and a constituent has to be confidential and my constituency correspondence will go into an archive where it will be kept secret for a hundred years.

The nicest letter I had when I left the Commons was from a man who said, 'Dear Tony, I have just retired as a teacher and I want to thank you for helping me get a grant for teacher training college, forty years ago.'

The surgeries became almost like a psychotherapy session. One elderly man on crutches asked me to help him pro-secute his teenage son and, with gentle questioning he poured out a whole series of incidents. I asked him at the end, 'I wonder whether possibly you are a bit jealous of your son?' His attitude changed and he clapped his thigh, shook my hand and said, 'Mr Benn, I believe you are absolutely right.' He picked up his crutches and walked out.

I have given a lot of thought to the work of a local member of parliament and have come to the view that much of the casework fell into the same category as the palliative care offered by hospices. Support was needed whether or not you could actually solve the problem for a particular constituent. The people who wrote to me or queued up at my advice centres to tell me their stories, wanted to be heard and they wanted me to listen. Even the most conscientious member of parliament could not solve every problem because many of them were insoluble, but in listening and then taking up their case with the authorities, I was not only acting as a powerful friend to them, but also I was learning all the time.

People were very understanding if you failed, and I drew out of that experience, which was often painful and stressful, important lessons about social policy.

For example, the housing needs of people, young and old, have in recent years become acute. When I was first elected as MP for Bristol in 1950, we dealt with a serious housing shortage by having a massive council-house building programme and most, if not all, houses were met by public provision.

So, on the question of housing I knew that the acute shortage could be solved. In this way I became a socialist because of experience: it was not just the help that I was able to give but the fact that I knew that major changes of policy were necessary if needs were to be met and that market forces could not solve those needs.

Therefore socialism appeared to me to be a guide to what needed to be done and not some fierce ideological commitment forcing me to persuade other people that unless they believed in socialism no good could come for them or society.

I remember listening to a young socialist at a conference say during the course of his speech, 'Comrades, we are all victims of capitalism and we must smash the state.'

I was the next speaker and I said that it was an interesting idea, but I asked the audience to consider what would happen at my surgery the following Friday when a woman came and said, 'Tony, I am just eighty and my husband has died and I desperately need a bungalow.' How would she react if I said to her, 'Madam you are a victim of capitalism and you must smash the state'? I guess if I had said that to her she might have replied, 'Tony, that is terribly interesting but what are my prospects of getting a bungalow?'

I am afraid that those whose socialism is based on ideology rather than an understanding of society are going to find themselves engaged in bitter battles with other socialist sects whom they will see as traitors to the true cause and enemies who must be destroyed before any progress can be made.

In Britain there are many socialist sects, including the Socialist Party, the Socialist Labour Party, the Socialist Workers' Party, the Socialist Party of Great Britain, the Communist Party of Britain, the Communist Party of

Great Britain and the Communist Party of Great Britain (Marxist-Leninist), not to mention the Scottish Socialist Party, Solidarity, Respect and the Socialist Alliance.

I know and like many of the people engaged in these groups but their passion for purity and for control has, I fear, deflected them from their duty to be representatives and campaigners.

There is an absolute parallel with religious sectarianism. Historically, Catholics and Protestants burned each other at the stake; Methodists, Baptists, Congregationalists have competed for the loyalty of the faithful. This has led to violence and bitter hatred in organisations which are supposed to be promoting love.

Then, of course, there are the Sunnis and Shi'ites, Buddhists, Zoroastrians, and many other religions which in pursuit of their own high ideals have found it necessary to kill and maim those who do not share them.

I have come to the conclusion that everyone, everywhere at heart shares the same hopes and fears. When I was growing up my friends and I rarely met 'foreigners', but *you* grew up in a city where there *are* no foreigners.

This is partly because science has broken down geographical frontiers, and with the growth of the internet you can hear the same things wherever you were born and wherever you live, whether it is Hollywood or Bollywood.

Take sport. I have never been interested in sporting events since school, but the international competitions – whether it be the Ashes between England and Australia, or the fantastic spectacle of the world's athletes gathered in Athens or Beijing, and soon London – show us those who excel in sports competing peacefully and give us heroes and heroines from many countries who become real to us.

Art has always been international, for you do not need to speak the language of the artist to understand a picture; and with modern technology we can and do have the opportunity to experience the greatest works of art that every civilisation has produced.

Similarly music speaks to all of us, and that is one reason why the Simón Bolívar Venezuelan Youth Orchestra is so popular. Its founder has said, 'Classical music *was* by the minority for the minority, then by the minority for the majority and *now* it is by the majority for the majority.' A quarter of a million young people are educated in music in Venezuela.

We must include the numerous arts festivals that have grown up around the world, of which Glastonbury is the most famous in this country, because it brings young people together to hear great singers, artists and orchestras in a formula that is extra-territorial in that it is not a nationalist event. Indeed its loose organisation of people living in tents and moving about freely has almost persuaded me that anarchy could work, because the crowds are held together by their common interests, without needing police to control them.

Inter-marriage and, perhaps more accurately, inter-racial partnerships are already producing the multicultural children of the future for whom nationality will have much less meaning. Food is also global and, whereas when I was young fish and chips was the traditional British diet, now every cuisine in the world is available: people don't see their food as a proof of their citizenship.

Travel is a global phenomenon today and the move from sailing boats to jets has blurred those frontiers which featured in my childhood atlases. As for the information revolution, which has only just begun, over 60 per cent of the world's population has a mobile phone, Facebook has 200 million members and satellite TV, the internet and Google have transformed our perceptions of each other.

The world's religions teach us that we are part of the human family, but that can be statistically proved in a simple way.

You all have two parents, you had four grandparents, eight great-grandparents and sixteen great-great-grandparents. If one generation comes along every twenty-five years, you can calculate how many ancestors you have.

Going back one hundred years from your great-great-grandparents gives you 256 direct ancestors. One hundred years before that gives you 4,000. Beyond that you soon run into billions. In other words, we are all blood cousins many times over, whether we realise it or not.

I have no artistic talent but have found myself drawn to an interest in politics, humanity and the arts by personal experience, working with a retired professor, Roy Bailey, who is also a singer and guitarist. I have found that the political message combined with music touches people in a way that would not be possible by speech alone.

Believe it or not Roy and I won the BBC Live Folk Act award, although I have never sung a note in public!

On other occasions music has been added to some of my speeches and reached a far wider audience as a result. I have also been sent hundreds of poems and pictures and songs by people who thought I might enjoy them – which indeed I have.

Within three generations we have all become beneficiaries of a world culture which is binding us together in a form of artistic, sporting and human citizenship that may be the cultural basis of the global village you will increasingly inhabit in the future.

LETTER 9

That global village which I have already mentioned can be experienced on every London bus. People from all corners of the earth are momentarily brought together in one small community. Globalisation is a fact of life. There is no reversing the change that it has brought about. But I prefer the word 'internationalism' to describe what is happening rather than globalisation, which has tended to be used to justify the reach of the international corporations world-wide. For in the global village there are many religions, races and common problems that now receive attention.

A hundred years ago news of a famine in some far-off corner of the globe would probably have never reached you; if it did, it would be the result of a dispatch sent by sea, of interest only to the Foreign Office. I remember when I was a little boy on holiday at Stansgate, Essex, my father (your great-grandfather) was on the telephone, shouting. I asked my mother and she said, 'Father is talking to the Viceroy of India, in Delhi.' So I wasn't surprised that he had to shout. It was only later that I realised that he, as Secretary of State for India, was responsible to parliament for the government of India, including what is now Pakistan, Bangladesh and Burma. We once had a visitor from India – the Maharajah of Alwah – who gave me a turban and prince's outfit. He was later murdered.

Today a famine in Somalia or Ethiopia is a famine in your village. You hear about it at once, on television, through the net and on the phone. Over half the global population now uses mobile phones, and it is impossible to escape responsibility for helping to deal with famine, even if only because it and associated instability are a threat to the security of everyone. Globalisation has changed the world for ever. My generation must come to terms with it or be outdated and irrelevant.

But global power is not new at all, for the history of empires from the beginning of time has been about rule across the world by the strongest nations over the weakest in order to acquire resources, cheap labour and markets. This applied to the Greek and Roman empires, to Tamerlane's conquests stretching from Central Asia to the Mediterranean, to the Ottoman, the British and now the American empire; and the arguments in favour of imperialism were identical to those put forward in support of globalisation.

Indeed, when the war in Iraq is recognised even by the then chief American banker Alan Greenspan as having been about oil, the question arises: why not buy the oil from Iraq instead of invading it in order to get control by force?

The answer is that globalisation today manifests itself, as did the old empires of the past, in military-industrial might which is quite prepared to resort to violence if it thinks it necessary for the preservation of its interests.

China has already become a superpower, India is close on its heels, Brazil is big enough to qualify. This will fundamentally alter the balance of power in the world. In my lifetime I have seen the British empire disappear and its replacement, the American empire, begin its relative decline. In your lifetime American supremacy may be replaced by Chinese or Indian.

Neo-liberal globalisation is often presented, quite falsely, as the means by which the rich and powerful can help the poor; any suggestion that it is immoral or self-interested is rejected as crude propaganda. But the price is paid by the exploited workers, and often the environment, through degradation of the land. It benefits a very limited range of people, for there is no suggestion that the free movement of capital carries with it a requirement for the free movement of people. That would lead to social disruption and would be completely unacceptable politically.

Thus a company – feeling under threat and stretched by international competition – can close its factories in Britain and transfer them to India or Thailand or Malaysia, where overheads and wages are much lower, conferring a benefit on the shareholders and the directors.

But if workers in India, Thailand or Malaysia seek entry to Britain, where the wages are higher, they will be stopped by the immigration authorities and be sent straight home, denying them the right to maximize *their* income.

Internationalism has always been at the core of Labour Party thinking, and socialists have seen their responsibilities to working people in *all* countries – very often against the interests of their employers in the home country.

In the First World War opposition came from German socialists as well as British socialists and, although overwhelmed by the bellicose propaganda, their solidarity was paralleled by the alliances that united people against the rise of the Nazis in the 1930s.

Similarly, the anti-colonial struggles waged by Indians against the British empire and by Africans against the European colonialists and apartheid were supported wholeheartedly by the labour and trade union movement in Britain.

When your parents Stephen, Hilary, Melissa and Joshua were themselves young, the Movement for Colonial Freedom (now called Liberation) was the great campaigning organisation, much as the Stop the War movement is now. I was active in MCF, which supported the African National Congress against the apartheid regime in South Africa, and there were French, Belgian and other European socialists who gave similar support to their liberation campaigns, for example during the Algerian war.

I think therefore that globalisation needs to be redefined as modern internationalism, and modern internationalism forces us to see the world as a little spaceship in which all the occupants have a common interest in survival – and that survival requires cooperation.

Cooperation is not only morally right and necessary but an attempt to prevent it is neither possible long term, nor acceptable even to the powerful because they know that they cannot control the poor indefinitely. If they try, bloodshed will inevitably follow.

Communication has been transformed in a generation, whether by air or by airwave. The world is closer to our living rooms than Edinburgh or Penzance or Belfast were when I was born in 1925. Internationalism in practice does more to weld these disparate communities together at home than you perhaps may realise. Muslims who have been isolated as a result of propaganda in Britain now find themselves befriended, supported and encouraged by white socialists and West Indian socialists who live here alongside them, and this is the building, at home, of the foundations of what will be needed all over the world.

It is a lesson that your generation does not need to be

taught because you understand it already, particularly in areas where the school population is racially mixed. This may be one issue in which you, as the first truly mixed-race generation, have a great deal to teach your parents and grandparents, who may not have come to terms with what has happened, don't understand it and are frightened by it. You are lucky.

In our family of three generations we have Anglicans, Catholics, Congregationalists, Jews, Hindus, Muslims and Humanists and we all get on together.

I was brought up as a Christian, and as I travel through England by train I love to see the church spires and the towers in every town and village. I always look at graves to see how old their inhabitants were when they died and visualise the people who loved them.

Christianity provided me with a set of moral values and a series of comforting rituals that covered birth, marriage and death. The hymns were uplifting; and the festivals at Christmas, Easter and Whitsun were the focus of much of the year.

The Bible stories were exciting: David and Goliath, Daniel in the lions' den, Moses and the Ten Commandments, Jonah and the whale, Job's plagues.

Jesus the man interested me because of his teaching and, although the horrifying account of the crucifixion is the centrepiece of the New Testament, it was only part of the story, and not one on which I ever focused greatly.

Christianity helped to answer some of the mysteries of life and death and provided me with the reassurance that there was someone who loved me despite my faults. When I learned to fly, in the Second World War, my mother said to me, 'Underneath are the everlasting arms,' as if God were a spiritual parachute like the one I had on my back. Even today, if someone I love is in danger, I will naturally pray for them in the hope and belief that it will be of some help in their trials.

But the mysteries and miracles of the Christian faith I find less helpful and that came home to me very strongly in 1945. I was an RAF pilot based in Egypt and I was on leave in Jerusalem. I had an opportunity to visit the Church of the Holy Sepulchre, the site where Jesus was cared for after he was taken down from the cross. There, in the centre of the church around the site of the sepulchre itself, the different Christian sects were scattered around as if in some pious pie chart, each claiming their section of this sacred place – the Catholics, the Greek Orthodox, the Coptics and so on.

The Abyssinian Christians were so poor they couldn't afford a slice of the pie chart and lived on the roof of the church, but they celebrated Easter by marching round, drumming their tom-toms in a ceremony know as Searching for the Body of Christ, which somehow symbolised their isolation.

On the same visit I went to the Mount of Olives and was shown a granite stone with a footprint on it indicating Christ's last step on earth before he rose to heaven, which, given the nature of granite, seemed unlikely – as did the scenes in the various chapels. In one there was a statue of the Virgin Mary from whose breasts milk pumped out on certain special occasions and attracted the faithful to worship.

In describing this I am not intending to undermine the faith of those for whom these things are sacred, or even to venture an opinion as to their veracity, but only to record that when I saw these rituals and symbols, I felt released to look at the teachings of Jesus rather than the number of lepers he healed or people he brought back to life.

For Jesus was a prophet, like Amos and Hosea and many before him, and thought of in this way he is a very meaningful figure in the world in which we live today.

What Jesus said was that we are all brothers and sisters and should love one other as neighbours. As I have got older I have come to realise that is exactly what all the major religions teach: treat other people as you want to be treated yourself – the Golden Rule.

In the Talmud, Judaism tells us, 'What is hateful to you do not to your fellow men. That is the entire law, and all the rest is commentary.'

For Muslims, the Sunnah says, with equal force, 'No one of you is a believer until he desires for his brother that which he desires for himself.'

Buddhism teaches, 'Hurt not others in ways that you yourself would find hurtful.'

These are the same messages some of you would have seen on trade union banners when you marched with me when you were little.

This teaching is of crucial importance in the world today but unfortunately the structure of the religions have replaced the message, and these structures produce their own kings. We should stick to the teachings and be careful of those who claim the right to interpret them in order to acquire control for themselves.

Religious and political leaders shine a torch on the path they wish us to follow but teachers explode fireworks into the sky so that for a moment we can see the whole landscape, learn where we have come from, where we are and the paths ahead.

Put crudely, leaders steal what the teachers taught, and they would be happy to obliterate their teaching so long as their own power was held secure. Thus papal infallibility arose and is unacceptable to me as I was born in the Dissenting tradition. I feel equally resistant to those who tell me that God supports the war against Iraq or that bin Laden claims that those who do not accept his interpretation of the Koran should be executed. Alongside this is the ludicrous Zionist argument that Moses went up Mount Sinai and God gave Palestine to the Jews, as if he was a biblical estate agent.

Nothing was taught me that was hostile to other religions (ignorant though I was of them), but one political point that did lodge in my mind was that nobody – Pope, bishop, priest – had the right to tell me what I should believe and nobody has the right to tell *you* what to believe.

You must often ask yourselves whether it is possible to change the world in which you live. Given a population of nearly 7 billion people, it is understandable that you might feel impotent to change anything by your individual effort. But by accepting the world as it is you legitimise it and thereby become responsible in part for its iniquities.

There are four questions which, although simple, and even child-like, get to the heart of the problem and offer a way for adults to act.

Where there is injustice, the first question is: who gave one person the right to do harm to another?

That is a revolutionary question which is directed at authority itself and the sources of power which sustain it.

Then comes the question: what is going on? It is often a difficult one to answer but it is also an important one because if you do not understand a situation you cannot influence it.

The next question is: why is it going on? It forces you to think about the nature of society and how it works.

What can you do about it? is the most difficult but also the most important question of all.

History gives you examples of people who have challenged injustice.

First, there are the teachers who have attempted to explain the world: Moses, Jesus, Mohammed, Buddha and the founders of the world's religions, who have all tried to lay out some moral principles which should guide us in our lives. In this category you will also find Galileo, Darwin, Marx, Gandhi, Einstein, Tutu and all those whose influence has been felt long after the kings, emperors and presidents were forgotten.

What they said has been tested and proved to be influential.

The next group of people who have left deep footprints in the sands of time are those who have combined into movements and campaigned – sometimes successfully, sometimes not – but have at least tried. You can learn from their failures just as much as from their successes.

If you approach your life with these questions and ideas in mind, you gain confidence, and self-confidence is an immensely important factor: the rich and powerful have confidence in themselves because they have at their disposal the means to do what they want.

The least confident are those who have no wealth or power and see themselves as the permanent victims of injustice, actually persuading themselves that there is nothing that can be done to change those injustices.

In this sense confidence is a class issue, because the wealthy and powerful convey their confidence to their own children, and nowhere is this more apparent than in the private educational system. That is why the comprehensive system is so important – it instills confidence in the working-class children who form the majority of its pupils.

What has always frightened the rich and powerful has been the appearance from among the oppressed of self-confident leaders who prove their strength by organising in a way that could alter the balance of power.

In the days of the empire such people were dismissed as 'uppity natives', just as working class leaders in the trade union movement have been condemned for questioning the existing power structure.

This is why encouragement is the most important thing that can be given: a teacher at school who offers encouragement gives his pupils the faith to carry on, and the old should encourage the young rather than complain and put them down.

LETTER 12

As you all know very well, I am an amateur inventor and am excited and intrigued by gadgets and devices which save time and effort. My latest invention is a stool attached to a suitcase, which represents the only safe seat left in the Labour Party.

Inventors have always fascinated and enthused me. From the sail to the mobile phone, the capacity of mankind for innovation is remarkable.

One of the most common mistakes made about socialists is that because they are suspicious of multinational corporations, they also somehow dislike enterprise.

I say this with some feeling because your great-great grandfather – John Benn – had a great talent for drawing, set up a magazine and founded a publishing enterprise called Benn Brothers. Uncle Ernest took it over, and wrote a book called *Confessions of a Capitalist*, which was published in a number of languages. Although if you read it now, he sounds like an early Thatcherite, it was his imagination that made the company possible.

Innovation is difficult in a bureaucracy where all decisions have to be cleared from above, where it is easier to say 'No, you can't,' than 'Yes, we can'. It is no surprise that so many inventors feel that they are persecuted by those with authority, who are not interested in change.

Put quite simply, anyone who produces a new concept or

product that is successful is automatically outdating all the others that previously existed rendering them obsolete, and that is not popular.

When socialists talk of workers, they must necessarily include small businesses, not only the ones that produce new ideas, but also the shopkeepers and organisations that meet most of your daily needs, and are run by people who work very hard, whether in a newsagent or a small engineering factory and do not have teams of accountants and public relations officers to market their goods.

The small business that innovates, develops and markets new products – as Nahal will know – or meets local needs efficiently, has to be regarded as the pioneer of the new technology and deserves public support and indeed backing from the labour movement.

A real political problem arises when it gets so big that it becomes a force of its own, using its influence to control governments. This is even more true of multinational corporations that have no local roots and are rich enough and strong enough to campaign to protect their economic interests against governments and parties that are much less well financed.

Where corporations run what are essentially public services, such as banks, fuel and power industries, and the basic transport infrastructure, I think there is an overwhelming case for public ownership, which is the only way of making them accountable. That is why in 1945 they were taken over, re-equipped with public money and operated in the interests of the public.

Bureaucracy in its most acute form, however, became

endemic in the public sector. How to establish democratic control over public organisations – in this country and across the world – is a crucial challenge.

Keir Hardie said in the early part of the last century, 'We have won political democracy and now we must go for industrial democracy.'

The public services and nationalised industries have often been criticised for being little more than 'state capitalism', when all that happened was that the nature of the enterprise moved from private to public ownership. William Straker, the Northumberland miners' leader, who sat on the Sankey Commission after the First World War, warned:

> Any administration of the mines under nationalization
> must not leave the mineworker in the position of a
> mere wage-earner whose sole energies are directed
> by the will of another. He must have a share in the
> management of the industry in which he is
> engaged, and understand all about the purpose and
> destination of the product he is producing . . . he
> must feel that the industry is run by him in order
> to produce coal for the use of the community
> instead of profit for the few people. Just as we are
> making political democracy world-wide, so we must
> have industrial democracy, in order that men may
> be free.

I greatly wish the trade union movement itself would take up the issue of industrial democracy because it would win a lot of support and could motivate society in a way that allowed the nation's genius to be tapped to meet the national interest. As you all face this huge economic crisis worldwide, you can never solve the problems it has caused if you cannot engage the enthusiasm of the people to make a go of the job that has to be done.

Family trees are immensely popular and give a sense of security and belonging. The family history of the nation is also fascinating.

The United Kingdom of Great Britain and Northern Ireland, to give its full title, is neither united nor great, but is a small group of islands off the north-west coast of Europe. It is a far cry from the days of your great-grandfather, who became an MP in 1906. Then, the British government and parliament controlled 20 per cent of the world's land mass, in which 400 million people lived – including Kenya, Uganda, Nigeria, South Africa, Rhodesia, India (with the area that became Pakistan), Hong Kong, Gibraltar, Australia, Canada and others.

Children who were at school then took all this for granted and it was presented to them as if it was absolutely natural and permanent – indeed it was explained that Britain carried the 'white man's burden', which was a responsibility laid on our shoulders to occupy and rule over the people who were in some way unfit to govern themselves. The 'sun never sets on the British empire' was the mantra, because in every continent of the world there were British colonies.

How we came to acquire the empire was not often discussed. It involved military expeditions over the centuries, made possible by the fact that the Royal Navy was by far the biggest in the world and patrolled the sea routes which safeguarded our interests.

It was because we were an island that the Royal Navy was necessary to protect us from invasion, and it was the strength of our industry that made it possible for us to build the ships and the guns and the goods which we sold to our imperial subjects, often made from raw materials acquired from their lands.

The arrogance of what we now call racism, which claimed that which those with brown, black and yellow skins were in some way inferior to us culturally, educationally and psychologically, was bred from this apparently natural order of things.

The wars we fought in the past 250 years were mainly imperial wars to protect our interests and to extend our empire wherever the opportunity occurred. We were told this would be of benefit to those countries we absorbed within our dominions.

Queen Victoria was given the title of Empress of India, suggested by Disraeli, and her son Edward VII was crowned in Delhi at a Durbar, a ceremony we invented, at which all the rajahs and maharajahs of India swore allegiance to him as King Emperor.

Although we were weakened economically and militarily in the 1914–18 war, our empire actually grew as we took over colonies that belonged to the defeated powers – Germany and the Ottoman empire. Palestine thus became a British 'mandate'.

The interest in this is more than just historical because it shaped the attitudes of those who were brought up during the days of empire – as I was. Some people still think the world was a better place when it was run by the British.

By the end of the Second World War, which left Britain much weaker, the anti-colonial movement within the British empire was growing in strength and demanding freedom and self-government so forcefully that it became impossible to resist. This movement had a lot of support in Britain itself, which enabled the transformation of the empire into a 'commonwealth' of nations, achieved without the bloodshed seen in Algeria and Vietnam, where the French tried to hang on to their colonial possessions by force.

Meanwhile, American imperial power was growing apace made possible by their economic strength, their population and their aim to make the world answerable to them.

As the American empire grew it was very hostile to the remains of the British empire, partly out of the historical memory of the American revolution which liberated the American colonies and established the United States, and partly because as Britain declined, America saw an opportunity to fill the vacuum that was created. Even in 1956 President Eisenhower secured the defeat of Britain in the Suez war because he saw that, until Britain was removed from the Middle East, US power could not take over.

Today Britain has little power world-wide, and in truth when Britain joined the Common Market in 1973 (which went on to become the European Union), this country became almost a colony of Brussels, in a union that the President of the Commission, José Barroso, has called a 'non-imperial empire'. Today you take the EU for granted and at school you are no doubt taught its merits and its role, independent of Washington or Moscow or Beijing, with its own NATO forces (albeit under American command), which Europhiles hope will lead to a European army controlled by a European government, in which non-elected commissioners hold more power than elected ministers.

So great is the change that it may be almost impossible for you to take on board the difference between your grandparents' world and your own, and vice versa. Although no one wants to go back to the days when Britain 'ruled the waves' – nor could such a thing be imagined – the attitude of the old to the world in which you live is still influenced by that memory.

Far-right parties based on racial factors because of these changes may appeal less to the young, whereas some middle-aged and elderly people still feel uncomfortable about immigration by people from countries with a different colour or tradition or lifestyle. For them globalisation is potentially destabilising and threatening, whereas for the young it has been partially transformed into internationalism. Oppressed peoples learn they have something in common with those in other countries, so that a world public opinion is beginning to evolve.

If you are to strengthen these new movements of opinion you have to do it consciously and deliberately, beginning with an education system that teaches the history of other countries and civilisations.

No doubt new empires *will* emerge as America declines and China, Brazil, India and Africa rise to positions of power based on their developing economies and justified by them as their natural right to recreate their own civilisations. If new wars come about, you will find yourselves in the position of our former colonies and you may need to invent and join new freedom movements to ensure that the new empires do not deny you your rights of self-government.

LETTER 14

Having been to hundreds of polling stations in my life, I have come to regard them as almost sacred in character. With a stubby little pencil attached to a piece of string, voters can put a cross on a ballot paper that will remove an MP from parliament, or a government from power, without killing anyone.

There are people all over the world who would give their life to get rid of their government, and here you can do it with a pencil if you act collectively.

When a constituent came to me, when I was an MP, and said, 'Mr Benn, I *never* vote in elections,' I would reply, 'Thank you for telling me because, whatever I do or say, I know you will never vote against me and therefore I don't have to listen to anything you say to me' – and that sometimes had the desired effect! The point is that apathy does not damage those in parliament but cripples those who would otherwise be able to hold the powerful to account.

Holding the powerful to account involves asking five questions:

What power have you got?
Where did you get it from?
In whose interests do you exercise it?
To whom are you accountable?
And how can we get rid of you?

It was Churchill who said that parliamentary democracy is the worst form of government except all the others which have been tried. Put modestly like that it is still absolutely true. But democracy in the United Kingdom is under threat on three fronts, quite separate from the expenses scandal which has beset individual MPs.

When I was elected in 1950, parliament controlled 'the purse', i.e. the Budget; 'the sword', i.e. the army; and thirdly, parliament could not bind its successors because every parliament could repeal every law passed by its predecessor.

Today none of these is true. Our level of public spending – the purse – is limited by the European Central Bank, which we do not elect, and the framework of our economic policy is global, i.e. the IMF, the World Bank and the WTO. This is especially true today when the IMF is being given even greater authority.

Similarly, the sword – our defence policy – is subsumed within NATO dominated by the United States; the Americans have military bases here which they can use without the need of parliamentary approval and the technology for our nuclear weapons is supplied by the Americans. It is upon the Americans that we depend for the satellite navigation system that enables them to be targeted.

Thirdly, within the European Union laws are made by the Council of Ministers, on which a British minister sits, but once made they apply throughout the European Union without necessitating the approval of national parliaments, including our own. Our parliament cannot repeal individual European laws even if voters elected a House of Commons specifically committed to do so.

The British parliament is therefore no longer sovereign

in law and the British people who elect it are no longer able democratically and peacefully to restore their control, through parliament, of the purse or the sword or the statute book.

In short, Britain has now become, in European terms, a big local authority, and this is one of the factors which has led to a certain cynicism about us as a self-governing democracy, and raises doubts about the value of voting. Because if we are a democracy the people must be sovereign and the government must be its servant and not its master.

This is a problem which you will have to deal with one day.

If Emily, who is now a parliamentary candidate, is elected to the House of Commons she will be the sixth member of the family in five generations over three centuries to sit there. It is, of course, only since 1948, two years before I was elected, that universal adult suffrage was finally achieved.

But since then there has been a steady erosion of democracy, to which the party system has contributed. The party system has become a disciplinary system and in many ways the Commons is now treated as if it were a government department, with the leader of the House and the chief whip as its ministers and the Speaker and the clerks as its civil servants.

One consequence is that the public have lost confidence in parliament and when that happens democracy is in real trouble, because the secondary function of a democracy is to provide a justification for obedience of the law on the grounds that the people make the laws. If that justification no longer obtains, power will move back to the streets. So great is the scepticism and cynicism about parliament today that popular contempt of the kind which led to cheering crowds when the House caught fire in 1834, may well return.

In saying this I am sure that *most* MPs seek to represent their constituents faithfully and argue their case as and when the opportunity presents itself in the House. But we all know that the pressures brought to bear on MPs by their party leaders are very great and can be decisive where a dissenting member finds himself unable on grounds of conscience to support the party line.

Government ministers are subject to even tighter control than MPs because their employer is the prime minister who has the absolute right to dismiss them.

Indeed, in the course of my own political life, in which I have been selected democratically to be a candidate, *elected* democratically to become an MP, and *elected* by MPs to join the shadow cabinet, or by the Party Conference to be a member of the NEC, or to be its chairman, the only time I have ever been *appointed* is when I was a minister.

Stanley Baldwin said that power without responsibility was the prerogative of the harlot through the ages, but ministers now, for the reasons outlined above, have responsibility without power and that is one reason why so many people are sceptical.

Politicians are bound to indicate what they would hope to do if they are elected to parliament, and that is a perfectly legitimate means of securing support – but they are less ready to admit that it may be impossible to fulfil their commitments once elected.

Eleven years as a cabinet minister certainly taught me that lesson. I realised quite early that all governments and individual ministers on election find themselves locked into a complicated power structure which does not willingly cooperate with those who have been elected.

This factor is underestimated, but in my opinion is critically important, for if a minister uses access to the public to explain the problems he faces the public learns the realities of power while at the same time being alerted to the need to campaign.

I was radicalised by office and I quickly realised that just getting rid of one government and replacing it with another one in which I had office did not necessarily change anything. A most vivid example was when marchers shouted, 'Thatcher! Thatcher! Out, Out, Out!' only to discover that they had elected Blair! Blair! and little had changed.

There are also limitations imposed on ministers by collective cabinet responsibility, which is an understandable requirement in a team that has to work together. I was often defeated in cabinet by colleagues who did not share my view and who by a majority – sometimes in a cabinet vote – committed me to a policy in which I did not really believe.

I tried to overcome this problem in this way. First, by drawing attention to public pressures with which I sympathised and indicating in a speech that 'the government would have to consider these points'. Another option was to jump so far ahead into the future that it was possible to say, 'in years to come governments may really have to think about how they deal with this problem', which took my contribution chronologically outside the lifetime of the government of which I was a member. The third way was to make it clear that if I was outvoted in cabinet I would say that there had been a wide-ranging debate and this was the decision of the government, without giving the false impression that I was necessarily in full support of it.

These techniques of dissent were not necessarily popular with my colleagues but the absurdity of suggesting that cabinets are automatically unanimous on everything undermines credibility. In a cabinet of twenty-four people it *would* be incredible for everyone to agree about everything.

The idea that a dissenting minister has to resign every

time his views are defeated is absurd because on that basis half the cabinet would resign every week and if an election were called those same ministers would have to urge voters to vote for the government from which they had just resigned.

I think if members and ministers were more open about their work and more honest in their presentation of what is happening, trust could return and the deadly cynicism would be replaced by honest interest and involvement.

LETTER 16

When the United States came into being it threw out King George III and set up a republic, blowing up the medieval structure of class which still exists in Britain.

The legitimacy of that monarchy, which still exists in Britain, is based on military victory or conquest – whether by the Romans, William the Conqueror or the Wars of the Roses – and on the hereditary system in which the eldest son or daughter of successful conquerors has carried on the family line and possessions down to the present day.

This system is a constitutional monarchy, under which the people are allowed to elect the House of Commons but the Crown is hereditary and the Lords, which were once hereditary, are now ennobled by appointment, using the so-called Crown prerogative.

Here is the secret of the modern system: although the person of the monarch has no political power, the Crown has great powers and these powers are exercised in practice by the prime minister. That explains why every prime minister ends up supporting the Crown.

The prime minister appoints ministers, peers, archbishops and bishops by using the Crown prerogative and that same prerogative gives him or her the right to sign treaties and make a host of appointments – judges, police chiefs and army commanders. By using these prerogatives the Prime Minister escapes all responsibility to the elected House of Commons for the use made of them.

While the prime minister needs the Crown to be able to make these appointments, the Crown relies on the political system to protect and ensure its survival. That is the deal that lies at the heart of our system of government.

It is sometimes said that Britain does not have a written constitution, but of course it does and I can repeat it in full.

> I swear by almighty God that I will bear faithful and
> true allegiance to HM Elizabeth the Second, her
> heirs and successors, according to law.

Everyone in authority has, on appointment or election, to swear a similar oath. As a member of parliament, on each of the seventeen elections I won, I had to swear that oath, even though my allegiance was never to the Queen but to my constituents, whom I represented, to my colleagues and to my conscience. As a result, in order to sit in parliament I had to tell seventeen lies under oath. As a privy counsellor there was another oath in which I pledged myself to support the monarch against 'foreign prelates, potentates and powers', but this one was administered, that is read to me, and required no assent by me. It was like having an injection.

Those who have sworn that oath include Roy Jenkins, Neil Kinnock and Peter Mandelson, all three of whom on appointment to the European Commission had to swear another oath that they would not be influenced by the interests of any government in the European Union.

It is in this way that the Crown has accommodated itself to the development of political democracy in order to survive, by conveying upon prime ministers the powers of the monarch.

But the Crown's social role is still crucial, despite all the changes and reforms of parliament, because it continues to sustain the class structure of society: the dukes, marquises, earls, viscounts, barons, baronets and knights stand in their set place in the hierarchy, while under them is a lesser hierarchy which manifests itself in the mass of minor honours given to good and faithful servants: the recipients of CBEs, OBEs and MBEs – long after the British empire has gone.

So important is the Crown to what I call the establishment that the latter is ready to sacrifice a king to sustain the institution, as happened when Edward VIII was forced to abdicate because of an inappropriate marriage which it was thought might weaken public support for the Crown. And that could happen again.

When the British empire ended, and the Commonwealth was set up in a mixture of nostalgia and arrogance, the king or queen was named in perpetuity as the head of that Commonwealth – which is why the present Queen is Queen of Canada, Australia and New Zealand, and why the presidents of India, Pakistan and South Africa seem happy to recognise the continuing authority of the British Crown in the Commonwealth.

It has no political or constitutional status, and it is strange that the heads of other Commonwealth countries do not insist that the title Head of the Commonwealth should rotate like the presidency of the European Union.

And one day you may want to choose your own British head of state.

When I was a minister, I decided to hang a map of the United Kingdom upside down on my office wall, to give me a different perspective on the way Britain was governed. At that time Westminster ruled England, Scotland, Wales and Northern Ireland. And that is what the UK looked like when the youngest of you, Sarah, was born in 1996. But you all take the fact of a Scottish parliament, a Welsh assembly and the restoration of democracy in Northern Ireland for granted.

Devolution has, however, opened up many new dilemmas, which you will have to sort out.

It was right to have a Scottish parliament and a Welsh assembly (however limited it still is) but it is incredible that England was not given the same right; we now have the absurd situation that Scottish MPs in the House of Commons can vote on policies which will not apply to their own constituencies, while a United Kingdom parliament retains many powers that Scotland feels should be exercised by its own parliament.

There is now an overwhelming case for the House of Commons to become an English parliament which would legislate on English issues. Its powers would be comparable to those now enjoyed by the Scottish parliament, powers which should be extended to the Welsh assembly, which currently has a complicated and bureaucratic system of legislation.

How would an English parliament be elected? By proportional representation? I have always disliked a list system of PR which transfers power from the electors to the party leaders, who decide *who* should be on that list and in what order. Although it might produce a statistically balanced parliament in terms of party allegiance, it would break the essential link between the government and the governed based on geographical representation and accountability.

I am not in favour of that solution. I think the best answer is to retain the constituencies but use the single transferable vote (STV) system, which would allow minorities to put forward candidates without losing the right to have what may prove to be the decisive influence in the final ballot. For example, if you wished to vote for a Green candidate, you would be able to do so, and if their candidate failed your second, third and fourth preferences would be carried forward so they still retained influence on the final outcome. This would deal with the defects of the first past the post system of 'winner takes all'.

You would also need to elect a small federal chamber with responsibility for overall UK matters – such as defence, foreign and economic policy – acting much as a senate and bringing together the UK as a whole for these purposes. A radical reform such as this would inevitably end the House of Lords. The present House, which has become primarily an appointed body with no democratic legitimacy and is open to the corruption associated with patronage, would fade away. The idea of an appointed legislature is a direct denial of democracy.

The time has come to sweep away the whole nonsense. The old hereditaries can still hang on to their titles and enjoy what advantage society accords them. Apart from the absurdity of a social hierarchy, titles have no significance politically. In that sense the hereditary system has been moved into a harmless realm that may be comforting but has no real meaning in a world where money is what counts.

Members of the new senate could perhaps be chosen by and from the national parliaments in proportion to the strength of the parties in those parliaments. For example, Alex Salmond (PM of Scotland), Rhodri Morgan (PM of Wales) and Gordon Brown (PM of England) would be members of the body which would elect its own president, who would also act as the United Kingdom's head of state and represent the UK internationally.

To move in this direction would involve a major constitutional change that could only be approved by a referendum.

Reform would also have to apply to the constitutional monarchy, which could thus be liberated completely from its role and be paid to attract tourists.

There is one other reform which is urgently needed. The whipping system, whereby members of parliament vote according to how they are instructed to by the party whips, must be reformed. The legislature should hold the government to account and the government should not be able to hold its own supporters to account for expressing their views and for voting according to their own convictions. Three-line whips should be abolished except for major matters of security and foreign policy, economic relations or manifesto commitments on which an election has been won.

It is ludicrous to expect that on every issue however minor, every MP is obliged to vote according to the party line.

When there are free votes on moral issues (such as

euthanasia and abortion) the House comes alive and the electors take a greater interest and gain confidence in the process.

The executive must be held to account much more vigorously than at present.

I believe that this could best be achieved through re-establishing the system of select committees, which are potentially very effective, on a much more democratic basis.

The committee system currently receives more coverage than debates in the chamber of the Commons, and undoubtedly they do hold the government to account in a way that does not happen in the chamber. The Treasury Committee, for example, has been very effective in the aftermath of the recent bank collapses; the Public Accounts Committee, the oldest select committee, has a well established reputation and exposes government waste and inefficiency ruthlessly. The Public Administration Committee has proved to be a thoughtful and well-led committee dealing with some fundamental issues, such as the Equitable Life scandal, that might otherwise have been handed over to a Royal Commission meeting privately whose reports would be unlikely to lead to action.

A really strong select committee system could prove to be a very useful counterweight to the presidential system of government headed by the prime minister of the day, which in recent years has also effectively destroyed cabinet government.

For the committees to become truly powerful however, and for their reports to be taken seriously, they should be elected by MPs, under the supervision of the Speaker, not appointed by the whips, who currently reward loyal MPs and exclude those who are more independently minded. If the members of each party were free to elect in a secret ballot those they wish to sit on the committees, the power of the whips would disappear and the committees would enjoy the authority of the House to do their work, choosing their own chairman free from the control of the whips.

Nor should anyone underestimate the importance of local democracy. Two of your parents (Stephen and Hilary) served on local authorities and witnessed the destruction of the GLC and the centralisation of power imposed on other councils in the period after 1979. It has gravely weakened the confidence of the people that they have any influence on decisions that affect their lives. The domination of local government by the Treasury has undermined local initiative, and with the outsourcing of services some local authorities are becoming little more than holding companies whose job it is to appoint or reappoint private companies to do their work. The election of mayors with executive powers has reduced local councillors to mere observers of the way in which that power is exercised.

The conclusion I have reached is that the function of democracy is to convert the arguments that are first heard on demonstrations on the streets into legislation on the statute book and to be the buckle that links popular aspirations into practical policies.

The pattern of this progression has almost always been the same.

If someone comes up with a good idea – such as abolishing slavery, votes for women or the end of apartheid – the establishment ignores it completely. It is not allowed to feature in public debate.

If the campaigners carry on, they are denounced as being mad. If that does not deter them, they will be described as dangerous, and possibly locked up. The suffragettes were imprisoned and, in 1911, Prime Minister Asquith said that if women got the vote it would undermine parliamentary democracy.

If all these attempts fail to silence people, then there is a significant pause at the top. Finally you will not find anyone in authority who does not claim to have thought of the reform in the first place.

So if you are campaigning on a cause dear to your heart, check it out against this list and see how far it has reached. And never give up!

In one sense Britain is now at war. Thankfully we are not being bombed, but families are being driven out of their homes by repossession when they acquire 'toxic debt' and factories are closing because they are uneconomic, while the banks demand billions of pounds on the grounds that they cannot be allowed to collapse because of their importance.

I was about Daniel's age when the Second World War ended in 1945 and I am very interested in the idea of tackling this current crisis on a war footing.

When a country is at war the government of the day has to focus its full attention on protecting its own people and defeating the enemy. That was the basis on which we fought the Second World War. When the German bombers destroyed homes and factories we rebuilt them and we protected people from shortages by rationing. Cost was not a factor. No general was so tied to his budget that he had to suspend activities during that year to avoid a deficit.

People accept enormous restrictions on what they can do, eat and wear. Conscription is accepted. People in the Second World War were required by law to join the armed forces or, in some cases, to go down the coal mines, as the Bevin boys did, to maintain coal supplies.

The parallel between war and peace was clearly set out in the 1945 election manifesto of the Labour Party, which could hardly have been plainer in its account of the situation facing the nation:

> The great interwar slumps were not acts of God or of blind forces. They were the sure and certain result of the concentration of too much economic power in too few men.
>
> These men had only learned how to act in the interest of their own bureaucratically run private monopolies which may be likened to totalitarian oligarchies within our democratic state. They had and felt no responsibility to the nation. The nation wants food, work and homes. It wants more than that. It wants good food, in plenty, useful work for all and comfortable labour-saving homes that take full advantage of the resources of modern science and productive industry.
>
> It wants a high and rising standard of living; security for all against a rainy day; an educational system that will give every boy and girl a chance to develop the best that is in him. These are our aims. In themselves they are no more than words. All parties may declare that in principle they agree with them. But the test of a political programme is whether it is sufficiently in earnest about the objectives to adopt the means needed to realise them. It is very easy to set out a list of aims . . . What matters is whether it is backed up by a genuine workmanlike plan, conceived without regard for sectional vested interests and carried through in a spirit of resolute concentration.

Even Winston Churchill's national government was not unsympathetic to those objectives. In its last budget, in 1945, the level of personal taxation for the richest people in Britain was actually running at 95 per cent.

This was the background against which the idea of a national health service was developed and launched. Although the country was almost bankrupt the government went ahead with it and at the outset no charges whatsoever were made. An amazing achievement when you consider that even today America, the richest country in the world, allows 47 million of its people to exist without any access to health care.

A really determined government now would not just be bailing out the banks in the hope that the old system could be recreated and made to work again. It would be analysing those same needs for food, work and homes and would invite local authorities to make a list of what needed to be done in their area to make this possible – and would fund them to do so.

There is a strong case for a far higher level of taxation on the wealthiest people in the country, partly to help finance a plan but also on the moral principle that those who are not affected by the present crisis because of their wealth could be asked to make a contribution to share the burden with those whose lives have been shattered.

Prime Minister Margaret Thatcher promoted the 'Right to Buy' for council house tenants; we should adopt the 'Right to Stay' for those who are threatened with homelessness because they cannot pay the mortgage.

If this is the approach we are to take, the government has to argue openly for it and win support for it.

One of the greatest weaknesses of the Labour Party, even when it is in office, is never to be seen campaigning for what it believes in but campaigning for re-election. You never see banners which say 'Labour Supports Peace' or 'Labour Supports the Pensioners'. Mrs Thatcher, by contrast, genuinely argued for the wealthy who supported her. If Labour were to adopt such an approach it would, of course, be bitterly attacked by those whose interests would be adversely affected and it would be endlessly misrepresented by the media.

The Labour Party cannot expect to survive if it is not seen to be defending the people it was created to protect.

This is not so much a matter of ideology but of common sense and the central question in Labour politics can be simply stated in this way: 'Whose side are you on when the going gets rough?'

In short, just as in wartime people expect the government to support them against the threats they face, so in times of economic crisis people are entitled to expect the same. The crisis has now reached the proportions of war and you will want to be sure that all governments meet that expectation.

In the same year that Hannah was born, John Smith died unexpectedly. Who was John Smith?

Your generation could be forgiven for not knowing that he was the leader of the Labour Party before Tony Blair, so completely has John been airbrushed out of the party's history.

John was a friend of mine, and I, like most of the Labour Party, was shocked at his death from a heart attack in April 1994, having believed that he could lead us to a general election victory. But Tony Blair, Gordon Brown and Peter Mandelson concluded that Labour could never come to power unless it incorporated within its manifesto a commitment to the economic policies of the Thatcherite Conservatives – hostility to trade unions, restriction of local government and further privatisation of public services.

Between 1994 and 1997 New Labour was launched as a new political party. Clause Four, the commitment to common ownership, was repealed and Tony Blair was elected prime minister.

After three election victories based on a falling electoral turnout, during which Blair consolidated his hold and launched two wars in association with George Bush, Gordon Brown came to power just as the government was hit by the credit crisis which has created a totally new political and economic situation.

During fifteen years of New Labour, the Fire Brigades

Union disaffiliated from the party, the Rail Maritime and Transport workers were expelled for supporting some Scottish socialists, and the Communication Workers Union were faced with part privatisation of the Royal Mail, spearheaded by Peter Mandelson.

At the time of writing this one thing is clear – that there has been a serious alienation from the New Labour government of many traditional Labour working-class supporters. This reveals the old dilemma – should the Labour Party be a party based on the working class, a socialist party or just a new version of the nineteenth-century Liberal Party which played the game of in and out with the Tories.

These are the questions you need to consider in the years ahead.

What is the working class? The media traditionally showed the working class as white men in overalls doing manual work, led by militant trade union leaders.

But workers 'by hand or brain', as the Labour Party's constitution called them, include everyone who lives by selling their labour as opposed to those who live by the ownership of capital. The distinction between the earners and the owners is a real distinction that the present crisis has brought into the forefront of the debate. A managing director with a very well-paid job, told to clear his desk by lunchtime, discovers he is a worker too and shares their economic interest.

The internationalism of labour, combined with global communications, has produced the most fundamental change to have occurred in Britain, with huge political impact. There is now an established population from the European Union and former British colonies, and from other parts of the globe, that does not share the history of the Labour Party.

West Indians, Poles, Czechs, Italians, Spanish, Ghanaians, Nigerians, South Africans thrive here (just as many Britons have left to work abroad). This dimension to the political debate needs to be explored and may explain why the BNP grows in strength because they see their route to power as building on the fear of British people of losing their jobs. Indeed some European immigrants are openly racist themselves and feel threatened by those who come from the old Commonwealth which deepens the division the BNP hopes to exploit.

The Labour Party has an unparalleled opportunity to harness this international workforce and rediscover its internationalist socialist origins – or it will die.

As I write to you, the whole world economy is in crisis. Unemployment is rising, companies are going bankrupt, banks are bailed out and there is a growing fear about how this might affect our future and our security. As the Sustainable Development Commission pointed out, the current economic system is fundamentally flawed and cannot continue: a fifth of the world's population earns just 2 per cent of global income. More investment in public assets and infrastructure, sustainable technology and a reversal of the culture of consumerism were some of its demands put to the G20 leaders.

The crisis is a rerun of the 1930s, but this time it is global. The system that has got to be put right has to be workable everywhere if we are not to drift back to protectionism, rampant consumerism and the conflict that brings.

Hitler found a scapegoat in the Jews, communists and

gypsies, and put half the unemployed into arms factories and the other half into the German army.

During the war, when I was in the RAF, we had a discussion on life after the war. I remember one lad who said, 'In the 1930s we had mass unemployment, poverty, destitution, the means test – but we don't have any unemployment during the war. If you can have full employment killing Germans,' he asked, 'why can't you have full employment in peacetime, by building schools, hospitals, houses, recruiting teachers and nurses?'

That is exactly what we did after the war – we reconstructed our industry and built the welfare state. We did it by applying the same single-minded determination to meet the needs of peace that we had shown to win the war.

The broad post-war political consensus was supported by successive governments of different complexions until 1979, when Mrs Thatcher came to power. Her policies amounted to a sort of counter-revolution in parallel with the presidency of Ronald Reagan, who set out to destroy the New Deal of the 1930s.

Thatcher understood the Labour Party better than it understood itself, realising that its strength lay in a democratic tradition of free trade unions, independent local government and publicly owned assets.

She therefore declared war on the miners, who comprised the strongest trade union in Britain, for whom the solidarity of men working underground with the constant threat of accidents and roof-falls was paramount. The first blow by the Conservative government was aimed against people Thatcher described as 'the enemy within', when in fact it was coal on which our industrial strength was founded:

coal-fired factories, trains and ships that gave us dominance in the world economy.

Having beaten the miners by using the force of the police and army, she introduced a series of draconian trade union laws which were more restrictive than those of the Liberal government in 1906; then she strangled local government in London with the abolition of the Greater London Council; and began privatising publicly owned industries – railways, fuel, power, transport, water. It was a breathtaking reversal.

Thatcherism did not end with the defeat of the Conservatives in 1997; Mrs Thatcher awarded the new party an accolade. New Labour, she claimed, was her greatest achievement.

At the end of the twentieth century conventional wisdom had it that the trade unions had ruined Britain, that the market should be allowed to operate unregulated, that 'boom and bust' were over for ever and that government should keep out of public life. It was a view that the architects of New Labour endorsed, as house prices rose, giving the false impression that everyone was getting richer; as trade unionists, unable to better their pay by industrial action, were encouraged to borrow to improve their living standard; the banks lent money they did not have to people who could not afford to pay it back, introducing a form of debt slavery.

Thus the credit crunch came. We can learn from history because the conditions now are similar in some respects to those in 1945; Britain is bust, jobs are disappearing; the country is engaged in war and intent on developing a new generation of nuclear weapons which will cost billions.

Socialism explains the world and the socialist analysis of

capitalism is still valid, but I have never seen the job of socialists as imposing a Marxist ideology on other people. If you want to make progress you have to deal with practical problems in a practical way. But Britain cannot act in isolation; the solutions have to be global, and fair and must address the needs of the 100 million people who have been pushed into poverty over the last year.

*W*hen *some of you* were little you used to help in local or general elections, pushing leaflets through doors, just as I did when as a ten-year-old I campaigned in the general election of 1935.

Over the years of my Labour Party affiliation, I came to understand how the party was formed and what its political objectives were.

There were two elements: the trade unions, who wanted working-class representation in parliament, and the socialists, who wanted the evils of feudalism and capitalism removed. This dichotomy was reflected in the Labour Party's constitution, which called for a society that allowed working people to enjoy 'the full fruits of their labour' on the basis of 'the common ownership of the means of production, distribution and exchange and the best possible means of popular administration and control of each industry and service'.

The Labour Party has had an ambiguous relationship with the trade unions, which have largely financed it over the one hundred years of its existence. The unions have always been blamed for the economic problems of governments, Conservative and Labour, as if every trade unionist is longing to go on strike and every campaign for justice is a threat to civilised society. Trade union leaders were described as 'barons' – though barons are not elected – and as wreckers. When she came to power, Mrs Thatcher used that theme to destroy the mining industry and blamed the unions for all Britain's ills, arguing that the market should be allowed to get on with its work and that governments should keep out of the market and the state.

Today, in the grip of this latest global debt crisis, nobody but nobody is suggesting the trade unions are to blame. But the bankers who *were* to blame are being rewarded with massive subsidies in the hope that the market can be recreated.

The Labour Party is a coalition that has moved under different leaders from left to right. It is not a socialist party but it has always had socialists in it, just like the Church of England which has always had some Christians in it.

But Labour could not have come into being without the strength of working people and trade unions. There are many in the party – and I am one of them – who believe that without union affiliation the party would wither away and, like the American Democrats and Republicans, Labour and Conservatives would alternate in office without fundamental differences. That is exactly what New Labour is all about.

But those who look to the trade unions to save the Labour Party must also recognise that the unions are big organisations and are themselves a part of the establishment, engaged in patient negotiations to improve working conditions for their members without destabilising the whole system.

Trade union leaders look with suspicion on those who

are talking about fundamental changes to society. But the victims of the present economic crisis will inevitably make demands based on their own interests, and the question is does the Labour Party support them or not?

The twentieth and twenty-first centuries have witnessed appalling brutality, from the slaughter on the Somme, the Nazi gas chambers, the bombing of Hiroshima and Nagasaki, the killing fields of Pol Pot to the Iraqi catastrophe.

But up to this point we have been confident that such barbarism doesn't happen here and that British values must be defended at all costs.

For that reason, the revelations about the torture to which people in Guantanamo Bay were subjected, and about the process of rendition, both carried out with the implicit consent of the British government, have shocked us.

If someone is captured in a situation of conflict and is thought to have information that might be helpful in averting an attack by an enemy that would cause loss of life, the temptation to torture such a person and the justification for it are not hard to imagine. Human rights are brushed aside in war and torture is as inseparable as rape, plunder and civilian deaths.

The official response to these allegations is that the government does not authorise or condone torture, but that is not an explanation that should satisfy us.

If the government intends to be taken seriously it should be required to answer certain basic questions: does the government regard torture as an offence? What complaints of torture have been brought to the government's attention? How many have been investigated, and by whom? If any approval of torture has been established, what action has been taken to eliminate it? Who has ever been convicted of torture? When? And by whom?

These simple questions are as straightforward as those that might be put about murder, rape or theft; but, of course, the government does not accept them as parallels, because they know that torture goes on but it would be embarrassing to admit it. How has torture come to be accepted as normal?

Over the centuries Christians have burned other Christians at the stake for heresy, and the grossest forms of capital punishment – such as hanging, drawing and quartering – were long established as methods of punishment.

I remember my father telling me that in 1924 he went to a dinner to celebrate the hundredth birthday of a General Higginson. Higginson described how *his* grandfather had been the governor of Newgate prison and at the end of a dinner party that *he* was holding lent a carving knife to the hangman to carry out the quartering of the body of a condemned man.

Torture is endemic in all societies whatever their ideology and it is only by public exposure that we can hope to end it; if we do not do so it will continue in all societies.

This raises the question of political responsibility for, although some of the worst tortures may have been committed by those acting on their own, in a democracy responsibility must be traced back to those who gave the orders, or knew what was happening but refused to stop it. Any definition of war crimes must include torture among the offences which could lead to a trial and conviction, as a warning to the world that it is not an acceptable practice.

After war service, as a student I listened on the radio to

the sentences handed down by the Nuremberg court which tried the German leaders. At the time, their execution by hanging seemed an appropriate response given the horrors for which they were responsible. The Nuremberg example has been followed by the International War Crimes Tribunal in The Hague and countries such as Iraq, where Saddam was hanged by his own countrymen.

Saddam Hussein is the only man I have ever met who was hanged, and when I saw his body dangling from the scaffold I wondered what would have happened if Nelson Mandela had insisted on the execution of De Klerk and Vorster for the crimes against Africans during the apartheid regime. If that had happened, it is not inconceivable that instead of the reconciliation which took place there might have been bloodshed in the years that followed.

This is how I came to see the importance of the work of Archbishop Tutu, whose policy of truth and reconciliation replaced war crimes trials as the best means of dealing with such offences.

For this reason I would be opposed to the trial and/or execution of the guilty for the war crimes for which I believe they were responsible during the invasions of Afghanistan and Iraq. There is another reason for taking that view, which is that we are all responsible for what is done in our names, if we live in democratic societies. I have to admit that, in 2005, I voted for a party that was headed by Blair and therefore must share some responsibility for what he did.

But if a United Nations War Crimes Tribunal was set up and in its judgment declared that war crimes had been committed in Afghanistan and Iraq, those responsible would have to live out their lives in the knowledge that they had been found guilty. That would be a more effective punishment than death.

War crimes tribunals tend to pin responsibility on one or two named individuals. If they are then executed this tempts us to believe the matter has been dealt with, without regard to the responsibility of others including, in Britain and America, the voters who put Bush and Blair in power.

Revenge is no basis for a lasting peace. That is why I have always been moved by the words of Bobby Sands, who died on hunger strike, and himself had been convicted of terrorism: 'Our revenge will be the laughter of our children.'

Earlier this year you may have read a news story about two submarines, British and French, with nuclear weapons on board, colliding in the Atlantic. It highlighted the huge risk associated with a nuclear defence policy.

The British government originally wanted a nuclear bomb that could be dropped from planes, but in time this was replaced by a nuclear missile which could be fired from a submarine – the Polaris system. Polaris itself was eventually replaced by Trident, which the government is planning to spend many billions on updating. One of the submarines in the collision was a Trident.

We are always told that nuclear weapons 'defend' democracy, but in reality they undermine it because no government is prepared to reveal the truth to its own people. Almost seventy years ago the Labour prime minister, Clem Attlee, who was generally considered an honest politician, never told the cabinet or parliament that Britain was developing nuclear weapons with the Americans.

In 1955 the first steps were taken to oppose these weapons. We set up the Hydrogen Bomb National Committee at a meeting in the Albert Hall, London, to launch a petition which was presented to No. 10 Downing St that Christmas. Later, the Campaign for Nuclear Disarmament began with a march to Aldermaston in March 1958. Aldermaston is the Atomic Weapons Research Establishment.

In 1958 I resigned from the opposition front bench, as

defence spokesman, on the grounds that I could not under any circumstances support the use of nuclear weapons.

The Non-Proliferation Treaty which was established in 1968 was intended to ensure that those states which had nuclear weapons would work towards nuclear disarmament and would cooperate with those states which didn't, attempting to help them with civil nuclear power (provided they did not use it to develop nuclear weapons).

As you know, this policy was not successful because China, India and Pakistan developed their own nuclear weapons and, although Israel still denies it, it is well known that it, too, is a nuclear-weapons state. So keen was Israel to prevent this news from becoming common knowledge that Mordechai Vanunu, who worked at the Israeli nuclear research facility at Dimona and reported on the programme, was imprisoned for many years. He is still not allowed to leave Israel and has become a hero of the anti-nuclear weapons movement.

When Ronald Reagan was president of the USA, Iran was actually urged to adopt nuclear power and it was suggested that the Shah, who was then in charge in the country, might be persuaded to adopt an American reactor, the PWR, and *supply* nuclear power to Britain.

When I was minister in charge of civil nuclear power in the 1960s and 70s, long before most of you were born, I was assured it was cheap, safe and peaceful. I discovered that none of those statements was true.

The problem of the storage of nuclear waste has not yet been solved but is vastly expensive, the accidents at Windscale, Chernobyl and Three-Mile Island demonstrated the risks, and it was only when I left office that I learned that – without my being told though I was the minister responsible – the plutonium from our *civil* power stations was sent to the United States for their *nuclear weapons* programme. In other words, every 'Atoms for Peace' power station in Britain was a bomb factory for the Americans.

I also discovered that an official in my department whose job it was to prevent nuclear proliferation, had secretly provided nuclear materials to Israel.

Now Aldermaston has been sold to an American company and the technology of Trident is an American technology – as will be its successor. We do not have an independent nuclear deterrent; the main political consequence of pretending we do is that it makes the British government absolutely dependent on American support. That may be one of the reasons why Blair went along with President Bush in his decision to attack Iraq. Had he refused, Bush might have cancelled the nuclear arrangements we had with the US.

Another argument against nuclear weapons is that they have proved to be totally ineffective in helping those nations that have them to win the wars on which they have been engaged.

The Falkland Islands were attacked by Argentina despite the fact that we had nuclear weapons – but the Argentines were not deterred.

America has nuclear weapons but they have not helped them in Afghanistan or Iraq.

Russia had nuclear weapons but it did not enable them to retain Afghanistan.

Israel is not protected by its own nuclear armoury from the rockets fired by Palestinian liberationists.

It is now becoming clear that some senior military officers regard Trident as a complete waste of money, money that should in their opinion be diverted to meet the needs of the armed forces for helicopters, body armour, tanks and other basic equipment. A field marshal and two generals came out publicly against the nuclear deterrent, describing it as useless against current threats, in a letter to *The Times* earlier this year.

Put crudely, in the nuclear age it is the guerrillas who win, and the suicide bombers cannot be deterred by the threat of death. Indeed they welcome it.

In a 2009 broadcast my friend Professor Peter Hennessy discussed the chain of command that would operate if a nuclear attack were to be launched against this country. He detailed everything that would happen between an attack being detected and the commander of the Trident submarine pulling the trigger to release his missiles.

In the course of the programme Denis Healey, himself a wartime officer and a very tough former minister of defence, said that under no circumstances would he have agreed to use nuclear weapons – on the grounds that 20 million people might have been killed.

This, in my mind, opened up the possibility that the peace movement should argue that they do *not believe* that a British prime minister would actually give his or her consent to the use of nuclear weapons. They should state that they had *such confidence* in the good sense of any such prime minister that we really need not worry about nuclear war.

In response to an argument of this kind it would be the prime minister himself who would have to 'reassure' the public that he *would* authorise the use of nuclear weapons, and I think many people would not believe him if he said that. And those who did believe him, knowing the consequences, would be less likely to support the continued existence of such weapons systems.

We are always being told that it is essential for our defence, while any other country that uses the same argument is denounced and threatened with military strikes as some Americans and Israelis have done against Iran.

I think it was Einstein who said the war that followed a nuclear exchange would be fought with bows and arrows. Against this truth, governments still plan to waste billions in future on Trident.

One final point. The very existence of nuclear weapons in *any* country destroys the basis of democratic accountability. The British government makes it a practice not to confirm or deny the presence or absence of British nuclear weapons anywhere in the world. Thus it prevents an elected parliament from asking relevant questions about the most important element in our defence policy.

This is why I joined the Campaign for Nuclear Disarmament and the Stop the War Coalition later, and why I believe that Britain would be best as a non-aligned country, developing a special relationship with the UN rather than the US. But that needs another letter.

You grandchildren are much 'greener' than I am and often berate me for my relative ignorance on green issues – especially Michael, who has a job as an environment officer in London. Young environmentalists grew up during a period of denial by the USA on climate change, but Obama has signalled a historic shift in America's attitude towards protecting the environment.

In his inauguration speech in January 2009 he said:

> . . . each day brings further evidence that the ways
> we use energy strengthen our adversaries and
> threaten our planet . . . We will harness the sun and
> the winds and the soil to fuel our cars and run our
> factories.

It was relatively few years ago that the environment was a cause discussed only by Greenpeace, Friends of the Earth, the Green Party and other 'single issue' groups. To that extent their influence and impact has been impressive.

A whole range of measures have begun to emerge and policies to be enacted in European legislation. Environmental issues are now discussed at meetings of heads of state.

There is a realisation that, if you do not tackle environmental degradation, the human race may find itself in very serious difficulties indeed. The world's population may rise from nearly 7 billion today, to 9 billion in twenty years' time. Food production will need to rise by half again, fresh water shortages are expected on every continent, not to mention the huge rise in energy use needed to power India and China.

The impact of climate change, as forecast by the scientific community, suggests that by 2030 the shortage of food, water and energy will cause major global upheavals.

The emerging policies have hitherto concentrated to some extent on energy because oil may have reached its peak level of production, and oil is a fuel of all our societies – not just at home and in industry but because of the vastly expanded demand for travel. When China, India and other developing countries demand the same rights of travel as you have, there will be a major crisis.

The remedies proposed concentrate inevitably on the saving of energy – everything from insulation to low energy equipment, to the recycling of waste and even more radical organisational changes in how society works. This new phenomenon is actually a very old issue going back to the beginning of time. Humankind has always had to earn a living off the land, and millions have died in floods or famine or by disease through man's incapacity to find a way of overcoming them.

Pollution has been a problem caused by industrialisation. In Britain Blake wrote of the 'dark satanic mills'; his poem 'Jerusalem' became a favourite hymn of the labour movement.

Over one hundred years ago Keir Hardie denounced the loss of the rainforests of North America, where already it was thought profitable to tear down the trees to provide grazing for cattle which kept the restaurants full of beef.

The Worldwide Fund for Nature has estimated that for

every man and woman in the world to enjoy the same living standard as the average American would require the resources of five earths, with their oil, food and water, to sustain them.

The environmental crisis is in one sense therefore a crisis of shortage. That is its dominant characteristic and poses a great danger, for it is inconceivable that the world could be at peace if millions were to be allowed to die in poverty at a time when the rich had secured their own supplies, using the military power that their wealth had given them to defend themselves.

Put simply, if there are ten survivors in a lifeboat after a shipwreck and they have one loaf of bread, there are only three ways that that loaf can be distributed: it can be bought by the richest; it can be fought for by the strongest; or it can be shared equally amongst the ten on board.

Contrast that with today's solution whereby wealthy corporations are to be allowed to buy carbon credits from the poor so that they can continue to consume disproportionately; and whereby land now used to grow food for a hungry world is being converted to biofuel production for the oil-hungry industrial countries, while food prices are rising.

The shortage of water threatens even greater potential conflict. The globe is covered in water but it is not drinkable without desalination. Massive plants, even if the world could afford to build them, would be very costly in energy.

It is worth considering how shortage has been tackled in the past.

Land is an immensely valuable resource, not least because no amount of hard work can increase the world's land area by as much as a hectare.

It is no accident that the French conquest of England allowed the invaders to redistribute land that had been owned by the Anglo-Saxons by giving it to their Norman friends; the story of Robin Hood, the Earl of Huntingdon, who lost his land to the Normans, is one example.

Later, the allocation of land became a very important political issue because much of our land was still in common ownership, and since the government represented the wealthy, it decided to allocate the common land to farmers, a process known as 'enclosure'. Thousands of Enclosure Acts were passed which impoverished the peasants who might previously have been cultivating the land, making them serfs on the rich men's farms.

I can well imagine the arguments used for the legislation: 'Large farms under strong management working for rich landowners offered the most productive way of growing food as compared to the previous confusion of peasants on common land.'

In Scotland, the Clearances had much the same effect. It was from these experiences that people came to see the importance of the land as a source of wealth and land ownership became political.

The men known as the True Levellers made the case for the common ownership of land, declaring in 1649 that 'The earth is a common treasury, it is a crime to buy and sell the earth for private gain.' Embodied in that declaration was a revolutionary sentiment, now again being hotly debated.

All empires seek to gain control of the land in the colonies they occupy. This is brought out vividly by Archbishop Desmond Tutu. 'When the missionaries came to Africa,' he said, 'they had the Bible and we had the land. They said,

"Let us pray." We closed our eyes and when we opened them, we had the Bible and they had the land.'

Even the resources under the earth, notably coal, fell into the ownership of the landowners on whose land they were discovered. It was a Labour government that brought the coal mines into public ownership in 1947.

Turning to shortages of food and of money: the Elizabethan establishment, no doubt fearing that the hungry could be dangerous, introduced the Poor Law, which provided for 'Parish relief' (funded by local communities), which gave the destitute enough food to survive. This was a measure of amelioration that did not tackle the real question of the unequal distribution of wealth, but it was enough to defuse the revolutionary potential.

Acute shortages arose during the Second World War, when German submarines had a devastating effect on the security of our food imports, which came by ship; the coalition government therefore took the radical decision to ration food.

In theory, it would have been perfectly possible to tackle the food shortages by raising prices so that supply and demand would be matched at a higher level, but this would have meant starving the poor, which was not acceptable, not least because the poor were needed to fight the war.

Looking back on the story of Second World War rationing it can be seen as an incredible act of public policy whereby, however wealthy you were, you could not get more than your allocated ration. Even those who were still wealthy enough to eat in hotels or restaurants were not allowed to spend more than 25p – then five shillings – on any meal.

One effect of rationing was to lead to an improvement

in the health of working class children, whose height rose by two inches as a result of their improved diet. So here shortage was dealt with by redistribution on a massive scale and, despite a few black market activities, was highly successful.

During the war we did not ration bread, but after the war the Germans were starving, and between 1946 and 1948 we rationed our bread to save the lives of those we had fought. That was a remarkable example of moral force through democracy.

The most recent example of rationing came in 1973, less than forty years ago, at a time of shortage of oil, when petrol was rationed.

Historical examples may seem very remote and indeed irrelevant to the global world in which you now live but it is exactly because the earth has shrunk that parallels become closer.

Today injustice in distributing goods in short supply could produce political and military consequences that would frighten the rich countries in the way that the poor in Elizabethan times frightened the rich into agreeing to the Poor Law.

No wonder the case for vegetarianism has re-emerged – not out of welfare concerns but for very practical reasons. We feed thousands of millions of animals every year so that we can kill and eat them; but growing food for the world's population instead of for meat might help solve starvation. I am not visualising the day when meat-eating, like smoking, would be banned, but we could soon face a choice of eating or not eating.

It may sound alarmist, but whether it is done to deter

the hungry from threatening the well-fed, or in response to a moral imperative to avoid unnecessary suffering, you shall have to begin thinking about a welfare world in which the UN lays down conditions that would secure a better re-distribution of such food as there is, impose the taxation necessary to secure it and indeed encourage the widespread development of family planning.

Whether the causes are man-made or not, and the costs of combating and adjusting are unnecessary, it would be, as the scientist Nicholas Stern says, 'very far from disastrous and we will have a world that is more energy efficient, with new and cleaner technologies and is more biodiverse as a result of protecting forests'.

The ending of waste, the sharing of existing resources, the protection of our earth for the future and the meeting of the world's human needs would in my opinion be your generation's best way forward to approach a crisis that is real and must be tackled globally.

You grandchildren lost your great-great uncle Oliver in the First World War at Gallipoli, and a great-uncle (my brother Michael) in the Second World War. He died at the age of twenty-two, younger than some of you, on operations as a bomber pilot. Many of my schoolmates were also killed.

Looking back on my childhood, war was a constant factor and people were 'called to the colours' from time to time to defend Britain and an empire which had been acquired by force.

In Westminster Abbey there is a plaque celebrating the achievements of our 'race', and when we captured Khartoum in 1898 – and killed 11,000 Muslims – the then prime minister, Lord Salisbury, said, 'The Africans will have grounds to thank us for what we have done.'

Those imperial wars are depicted in the website www.mapsofwar.com which has an animated map showing the empires from the Hittite to the British, rising and falling.

Religion was used to justify many of these wars, notably the eight Crusades. King Richard I, Coeur de Lion, launched the third to recapture Jerusalem for the Christians, only to be resisted by Saleh-e-Din, Saladin, the great Muslim warrior, with whom Richard agreed a truce.

In historical perspective, the twentieth century with the slaughter of the Somme and the huge losses and suffering of the First World War was just another phase of human conflict, and it is difficult to unravel in whose interests that war and the others throughout history were fought. The working classes of the United Kingdom and of the European nations certainly had no cause for conflict with each other, and the class analysis is one that helps me understand the existence of wars.

I have always been interested in the Christmas Day truce of 1914 when the British and German troops left their trenches and fraternised together, a move that terrified the respective governments and led them to order artillery to fire from behind the lines to frighten the offenders back into their own trenches and prepare for the bloodshed to begin again.

It was the suffering of the Russian people that gave Lenin the opportunity to launch the Russian Revolution and turn his back on the imperial war, and usher in a period of communist government. It is never mentioned now but Britain, America and France launched an attack on the Soviet Union against the Russian Revolution, though they had to withdraw in defeat.

In those interwar years between 1919 and 1939 it was the primary objective of the capitalist powers to destroy communism. Appeasement in the 1930s would be more correctly described as a sympathy for what Hitler and fascist regimes were doing to contain communism. Twenty-five million Russians died in the battles of the Second World War, which followed on fast from the First.

During the Second World War, Britain mobilised a wartime Home Guard known as Dad's Army, a civilian force of freedom fighters, under military command, which would have waged a relentless guerrilla campaign against the Nazi invaders had they landed here. I was a member of it at the age Hannah is now, before I joined the RAF. People laugh at Dad's Army but it was a serious project which allowed me to learn how to use a bayonet, fire a rifle, a revolver and a machine gun, throw grenades and use a primitive missile called the Blacker Bombard. If the Germans had arrived and I had seen a German officer having a meal in a restaurant, I would have thrown a grenade through the window and killed him. Would I have been a terrorist or a freedom fighter?

Let me put it bluntly to you. Those individuals who are defending their countries against America, Britain and other nations who invaded Afghanistan and Iraq are in exactly the same position and cannot be described as being in any way different from the soldiers we have fought in previous wars.

Within five years of 1945 the enmity between capitalist and communist countries hit Korea, NATO was established, mirrored by the Warsaw Pact of communist countries, and we were back to a rearmament programme that included nuclear weapons.

One of the by-products of the Cold War was that by the 1980s the Russians had invaded Afghanistan and President Bush the First funded Osama bin Laden to mount an Islamic counter-attack to fight the Russians.

The Americans also armed Saddam Hussein in order to fight and topple the revolutionary regime in Iran which, headed by the Ayatollah Khomeini, had succeeded to power after removing the US-supported Shah of Iran.

The outcome of this misguided strategy has been a series of conflicts across the Middle East and Asia, not wars against terror but wars against the countries and their peoples and there is no moral difference between a suicide bomber and a stealth bomber, for both kill innocent people for political reasons.

If Prime Minister Blair had refused to go along with George Bush in the Afghan and Iraq wars it is doubtful whether Bush would have dared to launch them alone, lest Congress, fearing a repeat of the Vietnam War, refused to support him – something the American electors now understand.

It is to be fervently hoped that President Obama can use the opportunity he has now for a clean-sheet approach to foreign policy which will make a fundamental contribution to securing peace.

My old friend Peter Ustinov once said, 'Terrorism is the war of the poor against the rich and war is the terrorism of the rich against the poor.' That just about sums it up.

Since the oldest of you was born in 1981, over a million people, many of them young, but also the elderly and the disabled, have died in the wars which I have described in earlier letters. The Middle East has featured in our history from the reign of Richard Coeur de Lion, whose splendid statue in Westminster shows him with sword outstretched, to the premiership of Tony Blair. With the encouragement of Blair and Bush Israel has conducted attacks on Lebanon and Palestine which have shocked even Israel's defenders.

Israel has always presented itself as being wholly concerned with the defence of its own security and over the years this argument has carried a lot of weight. More recently, however, Israel has absolutely ignored the United Nations, and been protected from formal censure by America, which has vetoed resolutions critical of Israel.

Israel will not recognise the existence of Palestine and will not talk to Hamas, the party which overwhelmingly won the parliamentary election in Palestine, but it demands that Palestinians recognise Israel.

Before the foundation of the state of Israel, Jewish terrorists were active, and after the state was founded it seized the West Bank by force; invaded the Lebanon where over 1,000 died in 2006, and still occupies the Sheba farms there; took the Golan Heights from Syria; built a huge wall to isolate the Palestinian communities, ignoring an ICC ruling that it was illegal; invaded Gaza, committing grave war crimes; and acquired nuclear weapons (a fact it still denies) – all in the name of self-defence.

Years ago, remembering the Holocaust, I supported the idea of a home for the Jews, and visited Israel more than once. But it is impossible to conclude other than that the Zionist case – that is to say the case for Israel as the biblically ordained and rightful home of the Jews – now dominates Israeli strategy to the exclusion of every other consideration. Now the Israeli prime minister and other leaders have questioned the viability of a two-state solution.

Any Jew from anywhere in the world can emigrate to Israel and be accepted as a citizen, but a Palestinian driven from his home is not allowed to return to it, and his house may well be allocated to an immigrant with no historical or legal claim to the area.

Critics of Israel are often denounced as anti-Semitic but, of course, that is totally untrue; Orthodox Jews have never accepted the biblical case for a Zionist state and have protested strongly against the state of Israel, while many other Jews have been bitterly opposed to the actions of the Israeli government.

One of the saddest parts of the modern story has been that the Israeli government have adopted Fatah and Abbas as the legitimate authority and Fatah has been ready to accept American support against Hamas.

Similarly, Saudi Arabia and Egypt, which have populations which are overwhelmingly pro-Palestinian, have been controlled by puppet governments who believe it to be in their own interests to follow American policy.

Such a system is bound to fail – partly because populations cannot be held down for ever in this way and partly because the Jewish people who live there can never survive without making a serious attempt at a peace settlement, offering to the Palestinians the rights Israelis claim for themselves.

There are those who believe, as the Jewish philosopher Martin Buber put it to me when I visited him, that the best long-term answer would be for Palestine and Israel to be part of a single state, free of racial separation and living together under a government elected by majority rule. Whether that happens or not – and the abolition of the Zionist state would be very difficult – the present imbalance cannot last.

The much trumpeted 'road maps to peace' have meant practically nothing, and can be seen now as an attempt by consecutive American governments to put the whole conflict on hold while they engaged in their wars in Afghanistan and Iraq.

President Bush's last ploy was the so-called Quartet comprising the UN, the EU, Russia and America, sucking in Tony Blair as an improbable advocate of peace. Bush saw Israel as his chosen instrument for domination in the Middle East and bolstered it with massive subsidies and arms supplies.

Israel is a major nuclear weapons state, armed by America. It exercises immense influence on American policy through its elaborate propaganda and intelligence operations inside the US. At the same time America is itself in decline, militarily and economically, and declining empires, like wounded tigers, can be dangerous.

No wonder the Middle East world is aflame with anger. It is important that Muslims should know that they have friends in Britain, especially on the Palestine question; hope-fully this knowledge will reduce the risk that this imperial conflict, like so many before, becomes a long-term religious war.

If Israel is to survive it can only do so by making peace with its neighbours. When history comes to be written, the Israeli massacres of 1,400 people in Gaza in 2008 may turn out to be the death knell of Zionism, which is the real enemy of the Jews worldwide.

In a message to the Iranian people, in his insistence on a two-state solution and in a speech in Cairo in 2009, President Obama is clearly repudiating Bush's strategy, trying to set out a new course for US policy.

I sincerely hope that you will live to see the Palestinians and Israelis living peacefully together whether in one state or two.

In my life I have seen the USA rise to become the most powerful empire the world has ever seen. It has dominated world politics now for most of my lifetime through its economic and military strength.

The Pentagon, which houses the defence chiefs, confirms that it has 865 bases all over the world – 268 in Germany, 124 in South Korea and, of course, bases in Britain. This figure excludes all American bases in Iraq and Afghanistan.

Under Bill Clinton, the Pentagon declared that its object-ive was 'full spectrum dominance' in land, sea, air, space and information. Francis Fukuyama wrote a book called *The End of History*, in which we were asked to believe that this new order would continue for ever – so we had better learn to live with it. With the end of the Soviet Union, the American century was proclaimed.

Foreign prime ministers pay court to the president in much the same way as the rajahs and maharajahs of India swore their allegiance to George V, King Emperor.

American culture has long dominated the entertainment market and American products sold around the world. And, of course, American power has boosted the worldwide domi-nance of the English language.

But there are factors which suggest that this empire is already in decline. The US is heavily overstretched militarily, its economy has been gravely weakened by the financial crisis and some of its leading industries, such as motor car manufacture, have had to slash their production and lay off workers.

The British empire was similarly predominant in 1900. Even in 1940 Winston Churchill, forever the old imperialist, speaking when the Blitz was at its height, said: 'If the British empire lasts for a thousand years, people will say "This was our finest hour."'

In fact the British empire lasted only another quarter of a century after that bold speech and, having lived in a crumbling empire all my life, I feel confident in reading the signs which are so clearly visible in respect of the American empire.

The US lost the war in Vietnam and is now losing its historic role, proclaimed in the Monroe Doctrine, in Latin America – eroded by the revolution in Cuba and the democratic changes in Venezuela and Bolivia.

The US cannot win in Afghanistan – no one has in recent times. And when Obama announced America's withdrawal from Iraq, it marked the end of a tragedy in which two presidents had inflicted terrible damage on that country and to the reputation of the USA.

What will follow? Inheritance of American power is likely to fall to China, India, Brazil or some other major country as it develops.

Even European leaders want Europe to be a great power. After the waste of blood and treasure in two wars the idea of the EU was to create a superstate – a non-imperial empire – reflecting the aspirations of the unelected political elite, but I doubt if it will come about. The EU is unlikely to challenge the power of India or China – but the aspiration has not disappeared from the chancelleries of Europe, where once kings reigned supreme over their colonies in Africa and Asia.

When I was about the same age as James, William and Caroline, I went in 1946 on a debating tour of sixty universities in forty-two of the United States, and the America I got to know then was welcoming and friendly and progressive – it was shortly after President Roosevelt had died. I therefore declare an interest in the special relationship.

It was indirectly as a result of that trip that I met your grandmother, who was from Ohio, and I became part of a wider American family. I have never shared the traditional left's hostility to the Americans who, under Bush and the neoconservatives, have themselves suffered because of reactionary policies.

The United States has a very rich radical history. In a speech to Congress in 1861 Lincoln said that 'Labor is prior to and independent of capital. Capital is only the fruit of labor and could never have existed if labor had not first existed. Labor is the superior of capital and deserves much higher consideration.'

In the 1930s America, under Roosevelt and his New Deal, was the only capitalist country in the world which moved to the left rather than the right. Roosevelt said, in 1936:

I have seen war on land and sea. I have seen blood
running from the wounded. I have seen men
coughing out their gassed lungs. I have seen the
dead in the mud, I have seen cities destroyed. I have

seen 200 limping, exhausted men come out of line – the survivors of a regiment of a thousand that went forward 48 hours before. I have seen children starving. I have seen the agonies of mothers and wives. I hate war.

And after the 1939–45 war President Eisenhower, himself a general, made a powerful radical speech:

Every gun that is made, every warship launched, every rocket fired signifies in the final sense a theft from those who hunger and are not fed, those who are cold and are not clothed. The world in arms is not spending money alone. It is spending the sweat of its laborers, the genius of its scientists, the hopes of its children . . . This is not a way of life at all, in any true sense. Under the cloud of threatening war, it is humanity hanging from a cross of iron.

Martin Luther King's dream charted the elimination of the formalities of racial discrimination although the realities remain in the USA as elsewhere. The peace movement in the US against the Middle Eastern wars has inspired parallel movements all over the world.

But the America of the twenty-first century, with its huge military budget, a foreign policy deeply hostile to the UN and a missile defence shield in space, cannot obscure the fact that the gap between rich and poor in America is wider than ever. Trade unions are systematically attacked and the corporations and mass media are immensely powerful.

Against this background how should we look at the election of Barack Obama, who offered real hope and made

'Yes We Can' into a great political slogan? He created a movement that elected him, that will back him if he does what he said he would and will hold him in check if he doesn't. But to have inherited a state apparatus set up by Bush and steer it into a new direction must be formidable.

As I sit here writing to you, Obama's overtures to Russia and Iran and his decision to meet Venezuela's President Chavez are hopeful; we shall see how they work out.

My point is a simple one: this is no time to be cynical; it is probably the best time ever to work with the real progressive America as partners in reshaping the world.

The biggest change to Britain's relationship with Europe since AD 410 will be made in your lifetime – by the Treaty of Lisbon. Yet none of you, nor indeed anyone in the United Kingdom, has been allowed to vote on it.

The British people have had a stormy relationship with Europe ever since the Roman invasion in 55 BC which left its mark on our landscape, laws and language.

In AD 61 Queen Boudicca galvanised the Iceni and other ancient tribes from eastern England in revolt against the occupation of the Roman governor, Paulinus. Seven thousand Roman soldiers were slaughtered, and it is a matter of opinion as to whether Boudicca was a heroine or a terrorist. Over 400 years later the Romans had to leave England because of trouble in Palestine, where their forces were overstretched.

The Saxons from Germany and the Vikings from Denmark left us their legacy before the Norman French arrived. Theirs was the last major invasion of the British mainland, in 1066.

The Napoleonic wars threatened our country in the early nineteenth century, and around our coastline remain some of the Martello towers built to repel the French invaders, who might have successfully crossed the Channel and added us to the burgeoning French empire. More recently, in two world wars we successfully resisted a German invasion. Given this history it is not surprising that the leaders of post-war Europe began after 1945 to think about how cooperation could replace conflict among European countries in future.

The project gained urgency because of the Iron Curtain between the West and the communist states which was drawn across Europe after the Second World War.

Tragically, our wartime cooperation with the Soviet Union (which had lost 25 million people in the conflict) had quickly evaporated.

The American Marshall Plan introduced after the war was intended to fend off socialism, particularly in France and Italy, and over the years helped revive European capitalism, where market forces dominated. Two institutions emerged in this post-war situation: the Common Market, to promote capitalism in the West; and the North Atlantic Treaty Organisation to protect it from the East. It was in part the recognition of this rapid transformation of Europe's strength in the world that reinforced the idea that the continent had to find a new role.

The Common Market, at first a mere trading arrangement, is now developing into a fully fledged European Union which is being asked to consider a European defence force to give it a military wing, a European president, and a treaty which would confer upon it the powers of statehood.

The EU has certainly to undergo a dramatic makeover if it is to survive, especially now it comprises twenty-seven vastly different nations with contradictory needs and demands.

The first basic right in a democracy must be the right of people to elect those who make their laws and the right to remove them; it is the only guarantee that those who make the laws will listen to those who have to obey them. Through membership of the European Union all the member countries have lost that right.

It has been calculated that a majority of laws enforced throughout the EU come from the Council of Ministers and not from the parliaments of those member states. A massive change has occurred in the democratic systems of Europe and has passed almost unnoticed because the founders did not want to emphasise it in case it led to a rejection of the Union.

For a start, the structure of the EU is complex and un-democratic. The commissioners are the key players in Brussels. They are an imperial bureaucratic elite who are not elected, cannot be removed save by an overwhelming majority in the European Parliament and therefore do not have to listen to the people over whom they exercise such power.

The Council of Ministers – comprising politicians from each of the EU countries – theoretically makes the laws under which the people of Europe are governed; but this law-making is done very largely in secret.

The third element – the European Parliament – is largely a toothless group of people elected by a tiny proportion of the electorates (turnout in the 2009 elections in *this* country was 34 per cent) of member countries.

Ministers who attend the Council meetings (as I did during my time as a British government minister) are not allowed to present papers for discussion but are limited to considering the proposals put to them by the Commission. It would be rather like ministers in Britain only discussing issues raised by their senior officials.

It has been the objective of the Commission in its Brussels

HQ to build a United States of Europe without ever declaring that to be its aim. This process has been subtly carried on first through the European 'constitution' (which was defeated by the French and the Dutch in referenda), and more recently by the Lisbon Treaty, which had precisely the same objective as the constitution but was presented as a mere 'tidying up' exercise.

The role of referenda in these massively important changes is significant because the parliaments and governments of Europe gain their authority from those who elect them – the people being sovereign.

In recent developments, the *sovereignty of the people*, which is the heart of democracy, has been subtly replaced by the *sovereignty of parliaments* who transfer the powers they have been lent by the people to those who are *not responsible* to the people, that is to say the Commission.

When the Conservative British prime minister, Ted Heath, took the UK into the original Common Market, it was without consulting the British people; a referendum held subsequently under a Labour government in 1975 confirmed our membership of the Common Market, and no subsequent referendum has been held here.

The Germans have never had a referendum; Ireland, under its constitution, is the only country that had a vote on the Lisbon Treaty – and rejected it.

Their vote in 2008 against Lisbon has been presented as if the Irish were out of step, whereas in truth not a single other member state in the European Union allowed its own electors to vote.

The European elite has now forced the Irish to vote again this year.

One of the great tragedies of this debate has been the way in which it has been presented as an argument between pro- and anti-Europeans. That is a complete misrepresentation of the real issue which is whether Europe is to be based on democratic consent or a new centralised bureaucracy set upon dominating a continent.

One ironic aspect of the Lisbon Treaty is the impact that it would have on the monarchy (to whom all MPs and privy counsellors have to swear an oath of allegiance before they can take up their position). In law, everyone, young and old, is a subject of the Queen; but our membership of the EU makes us all citizens of the Union and that includes the Queen herself, who has the right to vote in European elections, though I doubt she has ever exercised that right.

And if under the Lisbon Treaty the EU were to elect a president, then he or she will be the titular head of a Union within which the Queen is a citizen and she, like all of us, will be expected to recognise the supremacy of that president in all matters affecting Europe. If a British president of Europe visited Britain in that capacity and met the Queen at Buckingham Palace, he would not be a subject talking to his sovereign but a president talking to one of his citizens. This despite the fact that as a Privy Counsellor he would have taken the oath:

> To your uttermost bear faith and allegiance unto the Queen's Majesty; and will assist and defend all jurisdictions, pre-eminences and authorities, granted to Her Majesty and annexed to the Crown by Acts of Parliament, or otherwise, against all foreign Princes, Persons, Prelates, States or Potentates and

generally in all things you will do as a faithful and
true servant ought to do to Her Majesty.

The European Union is planning to elect a president who
would in effect become more senior than a British monarch.

As I see it there are three ways forward for Europe:

One: A fully fledged democratic constitution for a United
States of Europe could be possible, comparable to that of
the USA. Europe would then have a Congress and a president, all of whom would be elected by popular vote, the
commissioners would be abolished and this vast new venture
would be launched, openly and honestly.

Two: Alternatively, Europe could revert to the national-
istic Europe of earlier days, where conflicts over trade and
power could take place again and threaten us all, an idea
that has very little appeal. But the present European
Commission with its centralised directives could actually
cause such resentment that it led to a recurrence of the
nationalism we have experienced in the past.

Three: There is a possibility of a looser commonwealth
of European nations, including Russia, in which individual
countries agree to harmonise with each other by the consent
of their own parliaments. That would be a slower process
but it would have the merit of being more durable.

If we looked at Russia as a partner in building a new
Europe it would have dramatic consequences. First of all
Russia is too big to fit in the pattern of European feder-
alism and this would necessitate a serious reform of the
European structures, in order to develop a looser commonwealth where harmonisation by consent replaced diktat by
the EU Commission. It would also give Europe in this

extended form a great deal more muscle on the world stage in dealing with the US or China or India and this could be highly beneficial at a time when the economic crisis could degenerate into a splitting of Europe by nations no longer prepared to accept the rule of Brussels.

Whether Russia would be prepared to contemplate such a thing is another matter. With their relationships in Central Asia, Russia may well feel able to turn their back on such a proposal. But we ought to consider it and discuss it with them.

What lies at the heart of this choice is whether the people of Europe are to have any say in their future, and whether the crude propaganda that suggests that those who question the domination of the Commission and the Brussels elite are anti-European, is to be nailed. The delusions of the European elite that they are running an empire also reveal their view of the European peoples as their subjects.

Is it surprising that those subjects are turning against their masters?

Coming home in a troopship in 1945 I first heard the words of the United Nations Charter which was an embryonic constitution for humanity. It began:

> We the peoples of the United Nations, determined to save succeeding generations from the scourge of war which twice in our lifetime has caused untold suffering to mankind . . .

That was the pledge my generation gave to yours, and we tore it up when we invaded Iraq.

In 1919, when the League of Nations was formed, it was primarily composed of the imperial powers, who decided to make peace and set up a basic framework to help resolve their differences by peaceful means.

But the League broke down and in 1945 the United Nations came into being with bolder objectives under a Charter and with the Security Council and General Assembly to sustain it. The countries comprising the Security Council rotated and there were five permanent members – France, the UK, the US, Russia and China – who were given veto powers which still exist, long after the world balance of power has changed.

The liberation movements that brought so many colonial territories to national independence claimed membership of the UN as nation states – and were accepted as such. This was a very important change after the League of Nations, but it did not prevent the strongest countries from continuing their imperial strategies and making war when they thought it in their interests to do so.

The Suez war was one such, as was the Soviet intervention in Hungary, the Israeli expansion into Palestinian territory and most recently the wars led by the United States.

John Bolton, a former American ambassador to the UN, made it absolutely clear that the UN was seen as an obstacle in the pursuit of his country's interests, and the veto exercised by the Security Council five has prevented it from acting even when a clear majority favoured such action.

Representation on the General Assembly of the UN is unrelated to the national populations, with Luxembourg and Lichtenstein enjoying the same voting weight as China or India.

Also, international organisations which have emerged in the last sixty years, such as the International Monetary Fund and the World Trade Organisation, have absolutely no democratic legitimacy and are dominated by the strongest member states, notably America.

The arms trade, which poses a deadly threat to the prospects for world peace, is completely unregulated and multinational corporations that stride the world can play off one nation against another to maximise their profitability and power.

You live in a world in which globalisation is often presented as the solution to world instability because everything is interrelated and interdependent, but I regard that view of globalisation as little more than a charter for international capitalism to provide it with an artificial moral authority to do what it does, whatever the human and environmental costs.

There is no reason why you should accept a global settlement where the gulf between rich and poor is so wide and the threat of starvation so acute, and the military budgets absorb money that should go towards meeting human needs.

Your generation has to make an imaginative leap forward globally, as great as the Chartioto and the suffragettes made in the UK when they demanded the vote. Their struggles were eventually successful in wresting some political power away from the rich and powerful and secured significant advances in welfare and human rights.

Many people have written and spoken about a world government but it is world democracy which is needed and that will require you, the young, to plan for a democratic world organisation where the General Assembly of the UN votes according to the populations of the countries represented and the Security Council is answerable to *them*. If implemented now that would give Iran more votes than Britain and France.

It must also mean that a revitalised and democratic General Assembly, through the Security Council, would control the IMF and the WTO and lay down the parameters under which global business can work, including the arms trade, granting rights to trade unions and even specifying minimum standards of health and welfare which must be secured by international agreement.

To speak of this now may be regarded as wholly Utopian and unrealistic – in exactly the same way as those who demanded democratic reform in Britain were regarded in 1832.

The transformation that was secured in British democracy

was long and hard and sometimes bloody but it ultimately achieved justice and representative government.

Such a change would be a direct threat to the aspirations of the United States and the plans of other potential empires – including China and India – as they develop.

But it would give hope to people who out of desperation may conclude that their only hope to secure their basic needs is through bloodshed.

Such a worldwide democratic organisation is the only one that could offer any hope of security against chemical, nuclear and biological weapons which could not only kill millions but destroy the environment of the planet and the prospects for human survival.

A great deal of work needs to be done by the global generation. Britain could play a useful, if modest, role in redirecting its own foreign policy. As a non-nuclear, non-aligned state independent of American and European rule, we could try to forge a special relationship with the UN seeking to use our influence, along with others, to make it the instrument of international democratic control that we must have if the human race is to survive.

If such an idea were put to the world and campaigned for vigorously and honestly, I believe it would win overwhelming support. But the effort has to be made and it has to be made now by the new global villagers, of whom you are ten.

*M*any *idealistic youngsters* of your generation have become involved in campaigns for specific causes. Addressing a whole raft of interconnected problems seems impossible and single issues can also attract support from members of all parties.

But history has proved that single-issue advances are far broader in effect and scope than the original injustice. For example, the ending of slavery opened up a wider question of race and class and civil liberties in a way that may not have been anticipated when the single issue of abolishing slavery arose.

The case of the Tolpuddle martyrs, who established trade union rights, together with the Chartist pressure for parliamentary representation, combined into a major force for the creation of the Labour Party. The suffragette movement, which brought women into parliament, broadened the political debate beyond the narrower concerns of men and introduced issues on which women had a unique contribution to make.

Similarly CND, which began by opposing nuclear weapons, led to wider debates about war fought with conventional weapons and highlighted the waste of resources on military spending.

Campaigning on a single issue builds up experience which can and does extend to other campaigns, and the expertise acquired by organisations in tackling one problem is easily transferred to others.

Sooner or later, though, there has to be some overall organisational grouping to make change on a national scale, to defend class interests and act as an instrument for providing representation in parliament.

In that way candidates and MPs are able to be held to account for their overall actions. MPs owe their allegiance to their constituents, their party colleagues and their conscience and one cannot imagine a political system focusing solely on narrow issues, however important.

When you vote, you may find yourself having to choose between the lesser of two evils rather than the greater of two goods – but that does not make voting any less important. Millions of people in the world would give their lives to vote.

Can the Labour Party survive? I have addressed that question elsewhere, but you should never forget that every generation has to fight the same battles again and again for there is no final victory and no final defeat.

Even if *you* fail, your struggles can inspire those who have to do it in the *next* generation.

*U*nder *the anti-terrorism laws* you might well be stopped and searched by the police at any time. The film *Taking Liberties* shows how, little by little, British citizens have been stripped of rights which were regarded as inviolable. You are now the most thoroughly spied-on, recorded and monitored young people in the world. Your data could be included on the National DNA Database, the National Identity Register, the NHS Detailed Care Records Service, the Work and Pensions Department data-sharing, the Audit Commission's National Fraud Initiative, the Home Office's Intercep Modernisation Programme and the SOCA database of Suspicious (financial) Activity (which retains data regardless of guilt or innocence).

The slave had no civil liberties, nor the serf, and the civil liberties of the employed are limited by their dependent status. The democratic basis of rights introduced the revolutionary idea that the rights of the government are derived from the consent of the people and not the other way round. They have taken hundreds of years to secure, and without them there is no remedy for injustice open to the generality of the population.

We regularly cite the words of the Magna Carta which guaranteed the right to be tried by our peers, and although this charter was actually a deal between the king and the medieval barons with whom he was in conflict, the idea of trial by jury became embedded in our cultural history.

When it is breached, as it has been by successive laws allegedly to control terrorism, you are told by the government it is being done to protect you, much as the phrase 'protective custody' is used to describe the imprisonment of dissidents.

But civil liberties are not possible unless you are able to maintain privacy to protect them from state intrusion and this privacy was highly protected until relatively recently. Sixty years ago, a telephone could be bugged or a letter opened only after a secretary of state had personally signed a warrant to authorise it.

Today the government has secured the right to bug anyone's phone, gain access to their email and monitor their internet activities, and also to share this information with other countries in Europe. A European directive of April 2009 allowed across the board surveillance of internet usage and follows on from an earlier directive requiring telecommunications providers to store details of telephone records.

Indeed Europe is now planning to share this information with the United States. While all this is presented as a guarantee of our security there are very grave objections to it that need to be carefully considered.

First, the material they store about you may be inaccurate. Therefore your own record could contain false information. You will never know what is recorded about yourselves because it will be kept secret.

Second, if all your communications are recorded it would be very easy for anyone with access to use them for the purposes of blackmail, which gives the security services immense power over individuals.

Third, the information, as you know, is often lost or

published accidentally and, however careful governments may be, they seem incapable of maintaining the security which they claim they can.

I have no objection to a simple ID card with my name, address, photo and occupation. Very convenient to establish who I am. But the database is subject to all the dangers mentioned above and any government could use it for purposes quite different from the security arguments which they regularly use.

The right to trial by jury is also being eroded in a number of ways, not least by the readiness of governments to detain people without trial for a long period or keep them under house arrest ('control orders') and then conceal from those detained the nature of the charges against them. In its crudest form this is what Guantanamo is all about and with it goes the presumption of guilt. Presumption of innocence has always been the greatest safeguard against miscarriages of justice.

Most people recognise the importance of civil liberties and privacy but are reassured that only the guilty or the terrorist need fear these new powers; the rest of us need not worry. But for the reasons I mentioned, you are all affected as your liberties are eroded. If all your civil liberties were to be taken away from you in a comprehensive piece of legislation there would be great public outcry. But the government hopes that if they are reduced little by little you will not notice what is happening.

You must make it your business to watch your rights carefully and defend them vigorously against those who are continually trying to frighten you into giving up what has been secured by centuries of struggle. It is ironic that the

Convention on Modern Liberty which was launched earlier this year was inspired in part by the Conservative MP, my friend, David Davis's stand on the issue of imprisonment without trial and in part by the Labour government's authoritarian and anti-libertarian policies.

LETTER 32

Until we stop harming all other living beings,
we are all savages.
THOMAS EDISON

My mum and dad, and my brothers Mike and Dave and I used to go for a walk on Sundays. Our route took us up Whitehall and past a shop owned by the Anti-Vivisection League. There behind the glass of the shop window were stuffed animals, looking very realistic to a five-year-old, being tortured for medical research. It shocked me then as vivisection and animal cruelty do today.

From that moment I became concerned about all aspects of animal treatment, from vivisection to vegetarianism. Like all children I was fond of animals although I was never allowed to keep one as my father thought it was irresponsible to own a pet given his peripatetic lifestyle.

I always disliked meat and tried to avoid it, possibly because I could visualise the slaughter process. On holiday once I came across a slaughter house in a farm: on one side of the path the cows were milked and on the other side they were slaughtered. When I peeked in and saw blood on the floor I was appalled by it.

It was not until much later that Hilary persuaded Grandma and me to become vegetarians on environmental grounds. Neither of us ate meat again. The argument for vegetarianism on those grounds alone has become even more powerful as the world population rises and food supplies fall short of human need.

When the brain disease BSE hit the cattle and hurt the farming industry, more and more people turned vegetarian and it became acceptable rather than quaint to be quite open about it. One of the most interesting questions I put to primary school children is to ask them to raise their hands if they are vegetarian – usually about 10 per cent do, which is an indication of how strong that movement is. Then I ask the meat-eaters, 'If in order to enjoy your meat you had to kill the animals yourself, what would you do?' The meat-eaters look worried and a buzz of discussion develops as they confront the fact that the food they enjoy has been made possible only by the slaughter of animals which look so lovable and peaceful in the fields. In practice, of course, many animals are no longer raised in natural conditions, but in cramped factory units. A reduction in meat-eating would be better on humane grounds.

It concerns me that the animal welfare movement has been denounced as terrorism by those who benefit financially from animal testing. Some individuals have been convicted in the courts, but to use the word 'terrorist' to describe those in general who are protecting another species on our planet is an abuse of language and is an attempt to suppress opposition to the use of animals in laboratories by making it appear comparable with terrorism in modern warfare.

It was through my interest in this issue that I came to meet some of the scientists who have produced new and powerful arguments against using animals in testing and experimentation on the grounds that it is not scientifically sound and that the same research can be carried out as well or better by different methods.

Those who take this view are not animal welfare campaigners but scientists who believe there is a strong scientific case for their view, and so do I. The organisation Safer Medicines Campaign has drawn on a mass of evidence and its arguments are quite separate from animal welfare concerns. It believes that patients will benefit from medical research which is based on human biology rather than on the results of animal tests.

There is a powerful commercial lobby behind animal experimentation which seeks to justify testing on the grounds that drugs cannot be authorised unless they have been tested on animals. The scientists, whom I support, have pointed out that many of the drugs so tested turned out to create serious health hazards in humans despite appearing to be safe when tested on animals. Recent research has revealed why mice and rats are resistant to the adverse (and catastrophic) effects thalidomide produces in humans. The resistance 'involves a key difference between human embryonic cells and those of mice'. The same mistakes are being made again today in relying on mice for stem cell research. Who knows what key differences will be discovered after years or even decades of futile study?

Meanwhile, it is to be hoped that at the very least the number of animals used in testing (12 million in Europe each year, of which many are 'wasted' through lack of coordination and sharing of research) will be reduced by legislation in the next few years.

Humans and animals inhabit the planet together and we have to find a way to take cruelty out of it. Not just for the animals' sake but for our own. For who could engage in slaughter or torture without being diminished themselves? An activist wrote to me recently that in time people would look back in horror and ask, 'Was it really legal to do that to animals and did they really put people in prison for trying to stop it?'

You have been very tolerant and kind to your old granddad, who is a compulsive pipe-smoker. I have never taken any other drug; my generation and the one that followed did not experience the easy availability of drugs on the streets of Britain. The idea that people find excitement through drugs worries my Puritan conscience.

I recognise that drugs are widely used, but policies designed to criminalise them and abolish them by force of law, as well as eradicate their production, have failed either to reduce their use in this country or the production of opium in, for example, Afghanistan.

Prohibition in America in the 1920s, designed to make alcohol illegal and to imprison and punish those who bought and sold it, is perhaps the most vivid example of a policy that proved to be a total failure and had to be abandoned.

One of the reasons was that during Prohibition trade in alcohol was taken over by criminals and created a gangster world that did more damage than the alcohol itself.

A dear friend of mine, who was a High Court judge, told me that attempts to criminalise drugs have failed and were bound to fail. He pointed out that criminalisation has created the same underworld with all its associated dangers.

And talking recently to a former prison governor I found him saying a similar thing. People are convicted for drugs offences and then sent to prison where drugs are readily available.

I once asked a senior director of a major tobacco company what would happen if cannabis were legalised. He told me that plans had been prepared to enable them to trade in cannabis, as they did in cigarettes.

Of course some drugs are more dangerous than others but I have finally become persuaded that the case for decriminalisation is overwhelming. One of the reasons that MPs – with some notable and brave exceptions – are so nervous about coming out in favour of it is that they would be subjected to media vilification.

The drugs trade is now a huge international industry – and some economies seem almost to depend on it – run by groups who have acquired political power out of the wealth that they have accumulated.

One thing is clear: if drugs were decriminalised the trade would become more traditional in nature and the tax that could be imposed at the retail end could provide revenue to be used for social purposes (as tobacco revenue is today).

I put this in a cautious way because I have not felt able to campaign openly and consistently for a policy I think has become inevitable. It will yield benefits to society that hitherto we have denied on the grounds that enforcement of laws should be allowed to work.

My generation accepts that indulgence in tobacco and abuse of alcohol are a threat to public health – no one can deny it – but no government has yet felt able to ban them completely as criminal activities because to do so would provoke a huge outcry, would create thousands of prisoners and require a huge policing operation. For these reasons I have come to the conclusion that decriminalisation of 'recreational' drugs, which your generation find no more objectionable than alcohol or tobacco, should be introduced, combined with relevant public health warnings.

In reaching a final verdict I am very much guided by your views – I trust your judgement more easily than my own – on a subject which politicians, who will have to make the decision, are so reluctant to discuss honestly and openly.

*C*harles *Kingsley's most* famous book is *The Water Babies*, about the evils of child labour, which some of you when young yourselves will have read, but he also wrote a radical fictional account of the Chartist movement of the 1830s and 1840s. The Chartists made demands, and I have always preferred the word 'demand' to the word 'protest' because the latter suggests that we have 'lost' a battle and are able only to register our disappointment or disapproval. History is full of examples of people who demand rights and don't just protest against their absence – and it is the demands that the establishment has to take on board.

When Gordon Brown hosted the G20 summit in London in March 2009 the leaders of the world's rich countries were protected from the protests that took place against the economic crisis and the impact it is having on the world's poorest. Protesters were treated with a severity similar to that used against the Chartists in the 1830s and '40s when they *demanded* radical reforms.

At any time, in any country, the authorities base their claim to power on the fact that they are enforcing the law – very often a law that they have made and with little democratic legitimacy. It is also true that in every period of history there have been people who out of deep commitment to their conscience and faith have found themselves unable to obey the law and have chosen to defy it.

How should these cases be judged and what should our

approach be to the moral dilemma that a decision to defy the law involves?

In dictatorships the choice is relatively simple: those who do defy the law must expect to be punished by death or torture and imprisonment.

Autocracies are full of those who have made that choice and suffered, leaving behind a legacy of courage which has kept people's hopes alive. And historically many of the views for which they were punished have eventually prevailed.

In the societies which boast of being democracies, the choice is more complicated, for those who feel strongly that they must defy the law are told that 'You have the power to democratically change the law and therefore have no right to defy it.'

But it is more subtle than that. Although there is a legal requirement to obey the law, there is no moral basis for accepting an unjust law, and this is where there have been many examples of people whose conscience forces them to risk punishment. In your lifetime there have been many who have been prepared to go to jail in defence of nuclear disarmament, against the Poll Tax and for animal rights.

Gandhi is a great symbol of non-violent activism; he suffered imprisonment many times, but demonstrated the power of non-violence as an effective way of combating oppression.

Nelson Mandela was sentenced to life imprisonment for his struggle against apartheid, including violent action. Eventually he was awarded the Nobel Peace Prize and elected to the presidency of the country he had helped to liberate.

The Greenham Common women, many of whom were convicted for their campaign against nuclear weapons, were actually sentenced under the Justices of the Peace Act from 1361 for 'action likely to cause a breach of the peace'. Their offence was to hang teddy bears on the barbed wire at the nuclear base which contained enough weapons to wipe out the human race.

Not many of us – myself included – have the courage to take the course of civil disobedience whatever the personal consequences. For that reason I have never thought it right to advocate civil disobedience because I was not ready to undertake it myself, but I believe it is right and proper to support those who do take that action and I defend their right to do so.

Law-breakers on moral grounds have to decide what it is they hope to achieve by breaking the law. There is a distinction between the moral law breaker and the violent law-breaker who is engaged on a revolutionary challenge designed to destroy by force an unjust regime and substitute one that they believe would be better.

In societies that purport to be democratic most of those who take action are actually engaged in an educational campaign, hoping that the punishment they receive for what they have done will bring home to the public at large the moral basis of their resistance.

History is full of examples of those who have helped to persuade a whole generation that changes needed to be made in the law to bring it in line with their own convictions. The powerful, even if they have all the money and military resources to oppress, have always had to come to terms in the end with resistance based on moral principles.

'The state of the world is at the present day constantly changing: it is always becoming miserably worse, for he who spares nobody, and who is bent most on gain, is most beloved and most commended. Almost all the rich men are too avaricious; the poor man who possesses little must be robbed and spoiled of his property to enrich the wealthy.'

There are millions in the world who would endorse that view when a handful of greedy people helped bring capitalism to its knees. The words were written in the fourteenth century, at about the same time the first Poll Tax was introduced in Britain. The Black Death had killed very many peasants and as a result of the shortage of labour wages were tending to rise. The government responded with the first wage control policy in history, 'The statute of limitations', and introduced the tax in 1381.

This triggered the Peasants' Revolt which Wat Tyler led in a march on London and who, after approaching the king, was killed.

One of the most influential figures in the campaign was the Reverend John Ball. He said in one of his sermons:

My good friends,

Matters cannot go on well in England until all things shall be in common; when there shall be neither vassals nor lords; when the lords shall be no more masters than ourselves. How ill they behave to us! For what reason do they hold us thus in bondage. Are we not all descended from the same parents, Adam and Eve? And what can they show or what reasons can they give why they should be more masters than ourselves?

They have handsome seats and manors, while we must brave the wind and rain in our labours in the field; and it is by our labour that they have wherewith to support their pomp.

That moving sermon anticipated the writings of Karl Marx by many hundreds of years; it too, derives its power from its socialist appeal but also from our entitlement as Christians to be treated as brothers and sisters in a commonwealth that is based on equality.

The peasants were defeated but the words survived and can be seen as the first identification of Christian teaching with social action. Which is just as relevant today.

Another quotation which has helped me comes from Sir Thomas More, the last Catholic Speaker of the House of Commons before Speaker Martin. *Utopia* gave meaning to the word which still has significance today.

It is often used as a term of abuse dismissing ideas as being unrealistic, but without some vision of the future people are not prepared to strive.

Sir Thomas More put it very simply when he wrote,

People are always talking about the public interest but all they really care about is private property. In Utopia where there is no private property, people take their duty to the public seriously. No one has any fear of going short as long as the public store-houses are full. Every one gets a fair share, so there are never any poor men or beggars. Nobody owns anything but everyone is rich, for what greater wealth can there be than cheerfulness, peace of mind, and freedom from anxiety.

In that sense the foundation of the NHS was Utopian and in the war years before the NHS was founded 'fair shares' was the basis on which we rationed food to be sure that 'no one had any fear of going short'.

When King Charles I was overthrown in 1649 England became a commonwealth, or republic (long before America, France or Russia).

In our history books the period between 1649 and 1660 is described as the interregnum, the period between two reigns, to avoid using the word republic – implying it was an accidental gap between two kings. The laws passed then, including the abolition of the House of Lords, have been virtually obliterated from our school books.

The socialists within Cromwell's parliamentary army, called the Levellers, actually published the draft of a democratic constitution, which was called the 'Agreement of the People'. These were its key passages:

We, the free people of England, to whom God has given hearts, means and opportunity to effect the same do with submission to his wisdom, in his name, and desiring the equity thereof, may be to his praise and glory; agree to ascertain our government to abolish all arbitrary power and to set bounds and limits both to our supreme and all subordinate authority and remove all known grievances.

And accordingly do declare and publish to all the world that we are agreed as followeth:

That the supreme authority of England and territories therewith incorporate shall be and reside henceforth in a representative of the people consisting of four hundred persons but no more.

My interest in the 'Agreement of the People' arises because of the reference to the almighty as the inspirer of democracy; also because it was translated into French and became the basis of a republic in Bordeaux where they flew the Red Flag. Thus we can say that the Red Flag drew its inspiration from the Levellers long before it was flown in the French and Russian revolutions.

Under Cromwell the hopes of that constitution were never realised because he made himself Lord Protector and even abolished parliament, but the ideas had been planted and are as exciting today as they were then.

For me the real interest in the Civil War stems from the words of Gerrard Winstanley, the founder of the Diggers or True Levellers, whose pamphlet in the same year made an even bolder statement because it invoked the idea of inherent human rights.

In the beginning of time the great Creator reason made the earth to be a common treasury to preserve beasts birds fishes and man, the Lord that was to govern this creation; for man had domination given to him over the beasts birds and fishes but not one word was spoken in the beginning that one branch of mankind should rule over another.

And the reason is this. Every single man male and female is a perfect creature of himself and the same spirit that made the globe dwells in man to govern the globe; so that the flesh of man being subject to reason, his maker, hath him to be his teacher and ruler within himself, therefore needs not run abroad after any teacher or ruler without him, for he needs not that any man should teach him.

There could hardly have been a more revolutionary statement than that and it must have given enormous confidence to the people who read it.

The idea of God the creator was replaced by making Reason our creator, and it also included the first recognition of sexist language – 'every man male and female' – and it encouraged people to have confidence in themselves.

As with so many popular revolutions, the ideas released by the English revolution had a profound long term influence on thinking in Britain and the world and left many lessons for us today, even though the monarchy was restored and saved itself by making modest concessions.

More than a hundred years later Tom Paine said, 'My country is the world – my religion is to do good.' In a world where religious war is now a real threat those words lay the foundation for cooperation.

Paine also said, 'God did not make rich and poor. He made men and women and gave them the world to be their inheritance' – an early example of the environmental movement.

In 1825 Ann Wheeler issued an appeal on behalf of women against the pretensions of men to retain them in slavery; her words marked the beginning of the women's movement.

> Whatever system of labour, that by slaves or that
> by free men; whatever system of government, that
> by one, by a few, or by many, have hitherto
> prevailed in human society; under every vicissitude
> of man's condition he has always retained woman
> as his slave.

More recently, in 1891, Oscar Wilde wrote in *The Soul of Man under Socialism*:

> Agitators are a set of interfering, meddling people,
> who come down to some perfectly contented class of
> the community, and sow the seeds of discontent
> amongst them. That is the reason why agitators are
> so absolutely necessary. Without them, in our
> incomplete state, there would be no advance towards
> civilisation.

These words are part of our political inheritance. The last word must come from the women of Greenham Common, who marched from Wales to surround an American nuclear weapons base and to protest at the threat those weapons posed to humanity. I attended the magistrates' court where some of them were sentenced and one said these words, which always move me:

> The law is concerned with the preservation of property. We are concerned with the preservation of all life. How dare the government presume the right to kill others in our names?

The magistrates, having heard her plea, sentenced her and her colleagues to prison.

LETTER 36

When grandson Jonathan was little he referred to weather-cocks that he saw on buildings as weatherchickens. I often think of the weatherchicken when I consider the character-istics of political leaders.

I divide everyone, regardless of their party, into signposts and weathercocks. The signpost is someone who points firmly in the direction he or she believes you should go and, despite defeat, the signpost remains and is still there to guide you years later. By contrast the weathercocks don't have an opinion until they have studied the opinion polls, talked to the focus groups and been advised by the spin doctors.

I have absolutely no time for the weathercocks but I have always respected the signposts even if I disagreed with the direction in which they were pointing.

Mrs Thatcher was a signpost although I thought she pointed in the wrong direction. No one could accuse her of adopting a policy because a focus group recommended it, or a poll suggested it would be popular, or a spin doctor included it in one of her speeches.

She said what she meant and meant what she said and those who voted Conservative knew what they were getting. So those who voted were as responsible as she was for the policies.

'Say what you mean, mean what you say and do what you said you would do, if you get a chance,' is very good advice which I have tried to follow.

It is sincerity and passion in argument that have always influenced me and that is one reason why listening has been a better guide to me than reading. I find reading very difficult, when you think you have to decipher twenty-six letters, turn them into words and make out what the words mean! If you listen, you get a multiplicity of impressions which make a far greater impact. When I listen I ask myself questions: does he believe what he is saying? Does she know what she is talking about? Why is he saying this to me? Why is he saying it now? What does she want me to do? Why is it in his interest that I should believe him or has it got a wider significance?

All these impressions are important if you are to reach a conclusion yourself about the issue that is being raised. Of course the demagogue is a danger – he says what he believes and believes what he says, but his purpose may be self-advancement or to carry through a programme that is dangerous or harmful.

Using these criteria I have found it easier to make sense of what I hear and reach my own conclusions. For me this is the justification for the oral as opposed to the literary tradition.

It has often occurred to me that the great civilisations of the world were made up of illiterate people. Their skill was learned from the masters of the art – like those apprentices who watched the skilled brickmaker or engineer.

Bible stories were handed down orally, written up later and then described as the word of God which had to be followed and believed uncritically.

In my opinion, a book by itself can never rival an experience for the explanation of faith. Soldiers are often the most passionate against war because they know what it means: killing, violence and plundering assets.

Slaves revolted against slavery because of the brutality of a system that made them mere commodities to be bought and sold. It is no accident that great men such as Paul Robeson had the impact he had because he spoke from direct experience as the son of a slave.

Believing what you say is not just in order to win support but to maintain your sanity when the assaults by your opponents reach fever pitch, as they do when the ruling class and the media suspect that fundamental changes that would threaten their privileges are being promoted.

Harry Truman once said, 'If you can't stand the heat get out of the kitchen.' There is no doubt that progressive politics generates heat which tempts even the strongest to turn from signpost to weatherchicken.

LETTER 37

Young people are often considered as either idealistic or cynical and apathetic, while the old are often pessimistic. To my surprise and delight I am rediscovering idealism as I enter my eighty-fifth year.

Pessimism is understandable when brutality is all around, forever tempting you to believe that all is lost, that the hopes of youth for a better world have been dashed by experience and that those who still cherish those hopes are out of touch with reality. The human race, it is easy to believe, is just a collection of animals fighting for survival, power and wealth, and it will never adopt the policies necessary to build a better world.

It is easy for the old to use their experience to justify their pessimism by saying to the young, 'If you knew what we know you would stop all this foolish talk about building a better world and come to recognise that we live in a jungle where you will have to fight for your own interests.'

But this argument cannot be used against old people who retain their idealism despite the experience that they have had and indeed find that their own experience justifies hope and encourages dreams rather than destroys them. Jack Jones, the trade union leader who died in April 2009, and Helen John, the anti-nuclear activist come to mind.

All real progress throughout history has been made by those who did find it possible to lift themselves above the hardship of the present and see beyond it to an ideal world

– some Utopia that gave them hope and the strength to carry on.

This hope has been proved real by every struggling group: the trade unionists who were sent as convicts to Australia for swearing an oath to an 'illegal' union; the suffragettes, imprisoned for their campaign to get women the vote; the many leaders and movements which fought for freedom from their colonial masters; those who fought and defeated apartheid in South Africa; and now the environmentalists who are taking on the global establishment.

This is not to argue for the sort of Panglossian optimism that suggests that you should not worry because everything will end up for the best, because that is the very opposite of the truth.

But pessimism is a prison into which you incarcerate yourselves, removing any desire to join in meeting the challenges which face the human race, and thereby handing over all the power to those who now exercise it at your expense – and who have been corrupted by that power.

Every student of history learns about the corruption of power, but don't forget that there is also the corruption of powerlessness, by which I mean that those who think they have no power, from weakness, hand over the real power they do have to the powerful and thus become complicit in their own oppression.

Looking back on my life I have come to appreciate the crucial importance of encouragement, remembering the teachers who encouraged me, and the experienced MPs who did the same when I arrived as a youngster in parliament. When you are encouraged you can do so much better, and when you are put down you know the motive – to keep you under control.

That is why the powerful encourage cynicism because cynicism helps to keep people away from progressive movements. By contrast, those who believe in themselves and in the justice of their cause can only mobilise the movements to which they belong by tapping the fuel of hope which carries those movements forward. Hope is essential even if it is often dashed.

From the beginning of time in the hearts of everyone in every civilisation there have always been two flames burning, the flame of anger against injustice and the flame of hope that we can build a better world.

The best thing the old can do is fan both flames.

I am happy to confess that the visions I had as a youth for peace, justice and democracy worldwide have become more important to me now that I have had eighty-plus years of experience and I cannot be dismissed on the grounds that when I grow up I will see things differently.

If that is the only argument that I have to face then I am quite content to admit that I have still not decided what to do when I grow up. Even if I live to a hundred I would still be growing up – right to the moment that my body goes up in flames in the crematorium. And you grandchildren can then decide whether I was right or wrong.

LETTER 38

While I was waiting for a train at Paddington recently, a group of youngsters approached me with a placard saying 'Free Hugs' and asked if I would like one. One elderly lady was absolutely delighted, as was I, and responded with feeling.

The Free Hugs movement highlights the importance of affection in life and I am an honorary member.

It was not so many years ago that gay men and women were laughed at, attacked and sometimes beaten up just for being gay. And some religious fundamentalists still think they should be. One of the real and most positives changes that has occurred in my lifetime is the way young people accept homosexuality as part of the normal pattern of life; it has been quite a struggle to achieve that, considering the hostility homosexuality aroused and that the law made it a criminal offence to have a homosexual relationship.

Now all that has gone, although the churches have been slow in recognising it themselves – the gay bishop Gene Robinson from America was not welcomed at the Anglican Conference in London in 2008. The world is full of men who hate each other and when two men love each other the Church splits!

Prejudice against women remains strong in the churches and the Anglican Church is still wrangling about whether a woman can become a bishop while those who fought against women's ordination are mounting a campaign to ensure that they do not have to submit to the authority of a woman bishop.

Social legislation has helped promote the acceptance of many different lifestyles. The *respectable* world of my childhood has been swept away, thank goodness. Now, some people marry and some don't; some marry and have children and some marry and don't; some have children and don't get married; and others who love each other live apart because they value their independence while retaining a loving partnership.

In the 1990s there were the yuppies (the young upwardly mobile professionals) and then the dinkies (double-income no kids), now we hear of the skiers (older couples who like the good life and are spending their kids' inheritance). With property prices rocketing until recently, there were the home-loving kids, the kippers (kids in parents' purses eroding their retirement savings).

One of my favourite anecdotes is about the ninety-five-year-old couple who wanted a divorce and when asked why said, 'We waited till the children were dead.' Another couple decided to get married at the age of ninety-five and said, 'We don't want to but the parents insist.'

The one common thread in all of this is the need to *respect* other people and what they want to do. The only legitimate criticism is if these relationships damage other relationships or cause pain or hurt to those who are loved. If that happens the pleasures of some are bought at the expense of others. And, of course, for children, the stability, love and security, whatever the legal relationship between their parents, is paramount.

This idea of respecting different lifestyles has a huge

international significance because the lifestyles in other countries with other traditions may be entirely different and when people come to live here or we go to their countries there is a danger it may lead to tension.

From a religious perspective real problems do arise because some lifestyles would be considered a sin in many countries and the church authorities may reach a judgement on matters on which they have no experience, e.g. Catholic priests, imams.

The question of sin is difficult. It seems that religious authorities build authority on the claim that they alone are entitled to define sin and assert that if it is committed the person concerned might burn in hell or be refused admission to heaven.

This gets to the core of religious authority. The Congregationalists in Britain, for example, reject the presumption that God has conveyed his authority to others to speak in his name. They believe that everyone has a hotline to the almighty and need not depend on a priest or minister to speak on behalf of God.

Exactly the same problem arises when socialist leaders claim to be the sole legitimate interpreters of Karl Marx. When Stalin talked about the dictatorship of the proletariat, he was claiming the right to be dictator himself and anyone who disagreed with him could be executed – as thousands were.

Of course, during the Cold War Marx was blamed for what happened then but Marx had no more responsibility for events in the Soviet Union than Jesus did for the Spanish Inquisition.

Here we come to the very core of the democratic idea, which can briefly be stated like this:

All human rights are inherent and do not depend on being conferred by anybody who claims to have acquired superior rights which entitle him to bestow or withdraw the rights of others. We owe respect to others as individuals and groups and, to use a religious parallel, we should love one another as if each was a neighbour of ours.

LETTER 39

In this last letter to you all I have to admit that at my age I am beginning to think more and more about coming to terms with death. And young people must hope that they get old one day to avoid dying young!

Getting used to the idea that death is natural inevitably leads to the conclusion that it is also necessary, because the thought of living for ever would be a life sentence (if you know what I mean).

In contrast to the Victorians, our society talks about sex a lot but about death very little and, because of this, death is more mysterious and frightening than it ought to be.

I have become convinced that the right to die is a human right. Although there are problems about legalising it with no conditions attached, I assume and hope that my doctor will help me out when my quality of life has disappeared and I am a burden to myself and to you all.

In talking of old age I mean the period between a fit and active life and the moment of death.

Nature requires the fit and active to procreate, and the desire for sex and love are implanted in our minds to make that possible. (It has sometimes been said that men offer love in return for sex, and women offer sex in return for love, but it is a cynical way of looking at how real relationships are created and survive.)

When I got married my dad said 'Don't forget to keep a huge balance of affection in the bank because you will need it,' and how very wise he was because, as you will all find out, relationships involve stress and strain and temptation, and the possibility that these might lead to a break.

The concept of old age since even my parents' generation has changed dramatically. The sixty-year-old pensioner is the new middle-aged. The extraordinary improvement in living conditions and medical care and the increased longevity that has brought makes it even more absurd now to think of retirement at sixty or sixty-five as a process of winding down until the curtain falls shortly after. And that poses all sorts of social and ethical challenges which your parents, and you, will face.

The young and active will have to finance the hospital treatment, operations and drugs of a large stratum of older people. I have never forgotten Barbara Castle in the cabinet waving her finger at us all and saying, 'The standard of living we enjoy was earned by those who have now retired and we have a moral responsibility to see that the rising standards we enjoy are shared with those people.' Out of that belief came the policy of pensions linked to earnings, which was abandoned by the Thatcher government and never restored by New Labour.

What do the young get out of taking responsibility for the old? The answer is simple, for it is the sense of identity between the generations and the security that that sense of identity provides. I find it very comforting. But if older people are to be interesting to the young they have to be *interested* in the young and treat them with respect. I was talking about these letters at a meeting recently when a youngster got up and asked, 'What did you learn from *your* grandparents?' It was a good point! I certainly would not

have had the courage to write this letter if I had not bene-
fited so much from what my parents and grandparents taught
me. Apart from giving me their love and encouragement I
noticed that they listened to me and treated me with respect,
as I hope I do you.

Living as I do 'in a blaze of autumn sunshine' I realise I
have learned more from my children and grandchildren than
I did from my parents and therefore look with love and
thankfulness on the human family. It seems appropriate to
end these letters in a spirit of love and gratitude and sign
myself off,

With lots and lots of love,
Dan Dan

POSTSCRIPT: *The Daddy Shop*

Looking back at my family life I do regret having allowed my political work to take precedence over the great events of my own children's lives. This sense of guilt led me when Stephen, Hilary, Melissa and Joshua were little to invent a children's story which amounted to a confession. But it also made clear the strong bonds of love that bound me to them.

The story was about a busy father whose children decide to buy a new daddy. When I told it, Caroline would say, 'You are never to tell that story again because you are transferring your guilt to them!' I must confess I did tell it more than once and reduced them to tears! And here it is.

Once upon a time, there was a really happy family: Mummy and Daddy and their four children. Charlie was the eldest, a very serious boy, and the next was his sister, Annie, who was rather cheeky and had a reputation for being a bit of a troublemaker. Then came Bertie, who was very practical and could always solve problems. The youngest was Susie, who loved animals and was very affectionate and sweet.

They were an ordinary family and loved each other very much, all relying on Mummy to keep them together and look after their needs. She cleaned the house, did all the cooking and most of the washing up, supervised their homework and planned their holidays.

They all loved Daddy, too, and when he was at home, they had a wonderful time, especially at Christmas and Easter and when they went away for their summer holidays.

But Daddy was always so busy.

For example, Susie wrote a few poems at school and the headmaster asked her to read one of them at the school assembly.

She rehearsed at home and the whole family was so proud of her and made suggestions about what she should wear and where she should put the emphasis in her poem, and they all planned to go to the assembly.

All except Daddy, who had a meeting he had to go to so couldn't attend, and although they all understood, they were very disappointed. Susie was especially disappointed because her poem was about how much she loved her daddy and what a friend he was to her.

The same thing happened when Bertie was put in the school cricket team and was so good that he was made captain for one term. They were playing a championship match against a rival school.

Again the whole family rallied round and Mummy laundered his white shirt, Charlie scrubbed his cricket pads and Susie mended a tear in his gloves.

On the day of the match, the whole family were dressed up in their best clothes with their sunglasses on ready to cheer Bertie to the echo as he carried the team to victory – which he did. But, at the very last minute Daddy said that he had been called to a meeting which he had to attend. Although everyone understood, they were very, very sad, and Bertie in particular.

It was the same story when Annie was chosen for the school orchestra and was asked to play the lead violin in the Christmas concert to which all the parents from the neighbourhood had been invited.

Her rehearsing went on for hours at home, and it was her big day for she had been wondering whether she'd make music her career. So you can imagine the excitement as they headed off for Greenbank Primary.

Daddy, who was quite musical himself and played the piano, was especially proud. But about half an hour before they set off the phone rang and he took the call; and sadly announced that he couldn't go to the concert. He hugged Annie and wished her luck. But it wasn't quite the same. She was really quite upset.

Charlie loved school plays and since he'd gone on to Highland Park comprehensive, he had found a dramatic society which prided itself in putting on plays written by pupils.

Charlie had written a play that they decided to use in the Christmas drama presentation. It was a very clever play about a headmaster who fell in love with the school librarian, and the whole school attended the wedding and gave them a book as a present, which contained the manuscript of the play Charlie had written.

The excitement at home could hardly be contained because, of course they all knew the headmaster wasn't married and the school librarian was quite young, unmarried herself and it was quite possible that the head might have fallen for her.

The fact that Daddy couldn't even come to that was almost unbelievable. They wondered why he couldn't delay the meeting so as to join them all for this wonderful evening when Charlie would be the hero.

Although Mummy didn't mention it herself, the children did notice that she did everything in the house. The laundry, the cleaning, the shopping and mending their clothes. Although she had great interests of her own – especially writing articles for the local newspaper and gardening – she never seemed to find the time to do it.

But she was much too loyal to criticise Daddy.

One summer, when they were heading for a holiday in the South of France, Daddy turned up at the airport and said he'd been called to a conference and couldn't come. The family put on a brave face and waved Daddy goodbye as he left Heathrow airport, to go back to his office while they got on the plane.

On holiday, they missed all the things they would have done with Daddy and they sat about looking at magazines.

'Buy a new car this summer', said an advert and it described how to ditch the old car and buy a new one, which was all gleaming and bright and so much better than the battered old machine they had at home. They had quite a discussion about whether Daddy would agree.

There were all the advertisements for clothes with lovely pictures of what should be worn this winter by schoolboys and schoolgirls.

The idea that you could get what you wanted from a shop started a very interesting discussion. Charlie said one day, 'Why can't we buy a new daddy?'

Susie said, 'What a good idea!'

Annie said, 'Why don't we go to the Daddy Shop?'

Bertie promised to find out where the shop was when they got home and to do it as a surprise for Mummy, without letting Daddy know.

So one Saturday afternoon when they were all back home and together, the children said to Mummy, 'We're going shopping, will you come with us?' Just at that moment, Daddy popped his head round the door and said, 'I've got nothing to do, can I come with you?'

This was their perfect opportunity. Bertie showed them where the Daddy Shop was and they found it at once with a wonderful window display of models of all sorts of daddies – old and young, long and short, some dressed up in sporting gear, and one in swimming shorts as if he were about to plunge into a pool.

The man behind the counter was rather gruff, but when the children told him they were looking for a new daddy, he smiled and fetched a number of different daddies, like the ones they'd seen in the window. The children talked to them all and agreed the one that they really liked was the one who looked like the man in the window in swimming trunks ready for a dip.

They talked to him and he was kind and friendly and so after a little huddle in the corner to decide, Charlie went back to the man behind the counter and said that they'd like that New Daddy.

Their real Daddy hadn't been listening, because he had found a chair and was looking at some papers he had to read for his next meeting. Mummy said she had had to go home because she'd forgotten her purse.

The children asked how much they'd have to pay for the New Daddy. The man from the Daddy Shop said, 'Well, I'm prepared to exchange him for that man over there and I won't charge you at all.'

So the shopkeeper went up to their old daddy and said, 'Would you like to come to the back of the shop for a moment?' The children thought it might be a new meeting he could go to.

The New Daddy was so friendly and asked, 'Right, children! What should we do now?' that they said, 'Come on, New Daddy, we'd like to take you to our house!' He danced along the road – holding them by the hand at crossings, telling jokes and even singing a song. They were getting to like him already.

When they opened the door at home and saw Mummy there, they all shouted out, 'Mummy! Here's our New Daddy that we got from the Daddy Shop! He's promised to come to all our school events and on holiday with us and we think you'll like him very much.'

The New Daddy went straight up to Mummy and said he would like to help her clean the kitchen and tidy the books that were scattered all over the table there.

Mummy was really touched, and he did the job so efficiently that the place looked bright and cheerful in no time. When the New Daddy offered to cook the meal and wash it up she was delighted.

When Mummy asked where the old Daddy was, the children replied, 'We think he's gone to another meeting, and may be away for some time.'

So that's how the children got the New Daddy, and he was as good as his word. Always at the school, talking to the teachers, getting to know their friends there and their families, organising outings, taking them to the theatre and concerts and, throughout the autumn, helping them to practise for the football season when the cricket stumps had been put away.

And Mummy really liked him too because he ironed the shirts, tidied the garden and even typed up the articles she had to write whilst she dictated them to him.

At Christmas, the New Daddy said he had to go home to see his own parents who lived miles away.

He packed up his stuff, said goodbye to the children, shook hands with Mummy and set off for a month's holiday.

The children were planning their Christmas shopping and one night when they were all in the playroom, Susie burst into tears. She sobbed and sobbed and Charlie, Annie and Bertie tried to comfort her.

'Why are you sad?' they said, and Susie blurted out, 'I miss our real Daddy.'

Bertie said, 'You know Old Daddy used to help us decorate the tree and put up the Christmas cards.'

At this, Annie burst into tears too because she was reminded of the lovely bedtime stories Daddy told them, about life when he was a child and the holidays then.

They were all crying when Mummy happened to come in and asked what was wrong. So they told her, and she burst into tears as well. She said, 'Well, I feel just the same as you do, but I thought you liked the New Daddy so much that I had to agree to him.'

They were all hugging each other when Charlie spoke up. 'You know,' he said, 'there's a very simple solution to the problem.'

'What?' asked Annie.

'Well,' said Charlie. 'Let's go back to the Daddy Shop and get our Old Daddy back!' The children all leapt up and said, 'Let's set off straight away.'

And so they did. When they got to the Daddy Shop, the same gruff man was behind the counter, but he recognised the children and asked them why they'd come.

'Well,' said Charlie. 'Where is our Old Daddy, because we want him back'.

The gruff man said, 'I think he's somewhere at the back of the shop,' so the whole family – Mummy and the children – rushed to the back of the shop and began looking

There in a dark corner, sitting by himself, was their real Daddy looking very sad. They all just rushed up to him and gave him a million hugs.

'Why have you come?' asked their Old Daddy.

'Well, we all want you back,' they said.

Daddy's face broke into a huge smile and he jumped out of his chair and hugged them and said, 'I can't believe it! I thought I'd never see you again and I've missed you so much over the last few months.'

So that was it, and they marched out of the shop. The gruff man said, 'Where's the New Daddy because if you're taking the Old Daddy then I want him back!'

Charlie said, 'He's on holiday for Christmas, and if he turns up again, we'll tell him to come straight back here.'

They rushed out of the shop before the gruff man could say anything and raced home for a super Christmas tea with cake and jellies.

They had a lovely Christmas together and they sat and talked about it and what had gone wrong. Daddy said, 'I think I'm going to take a new job with normal working hours, and I'm not going to go on doing all those meetings.'

And the whole family lived happily ever after.

PS. Charlie switched the television on at that moment and they saw a prime minister leaving the door of 10 Downing Street and people cheering another man going in and waving to them.

'Why are they cheering?' asked Annie.

Mummy replied, 'Perhaps they're welcoming their Old Labour Daddy back!'